Exploring Hope in Spiritual Care

of related interest

Case Studies in Spiritual Care
Healthcare Chaplaincy Assessments, Interventions and Outcomes
Edited by George Fitchett and Steve Nolan
ISBN 978 1 78592 783 6
eISBN 978 1 78450 705 3

Chaplaincy in Hospice and Palliative Care
Edited by Karen Murphy and Bob Whorton
Foreword by Baroness Finlay of Llandaff
ISBN 978 1 78592 068 4
eISBN 978 1 78450 329 1

Hope and Grace
Spiritual Experiences in Severe Distress, Illness and Dying
Dr Monika Renz
ISBN 978 1 78592 030 1
eISBN 978 1 78450 277 5

Spiritual Care in Practice
Case Studies in Healthcare Chaplaincy
Edited by George Fitchett and Steve Nolan
ISBN 978 1 84905 976 3
eISBN 978 0 85700 876 3

Palliative Care, Ageing and Spirituality
A Guide for Older People, Carers and Families
Elizabeth MacKinlay
ISBN 978 1 84905 290 0
eISBN 978 0 85700 598 4

Spiritual Care at the End of Life
The Chaplain as a 'Hopeful Presence'
Steve Nolan
ISBN 978 1 84905 199 6
eISBN 978 0 85700 513 7

Exploring Hope in Spiritual Care

A Practical Theological Guide for Chaplains

Laura E. Shay

Jessica Kingsley *Publishers*
London and Philadelphia

The *Poem for Mom* on pages 56–8 is reproduced with kind permission from Noah Holman.

First published in 2019
by Jessica Kingsley Publishers
73 Collier Street
London N1 9BE, UK
and
400 Market Street, Suite 400
Philadelphia, PA 19106, USA

www.jkp.com

Library of Congress Cataloging in Publication Data
A CIP catalog record for this book is available from the Library of Congress

British Library Cataloguing in Publication Data
A CIP catalogue record for this book is available from the British Library

ISBN 978 1 78592 576 4
eISBN 978 1 78450 987 3

Printed and bound by CPI Group (UK) Ltd, Croydon, CR0 4YY

This book is dedicated to
Abigail Prestin, PhD
1980–2014

Contents

Acknowledgements

I would like to express my heartfelt appreciation to my friends and family who have supported me through this journey. I especially wish to thank those who helped to make this book possible: my spiritual director the Revd Karen Johnson (retired Episcopal priest), who helped spark my journey into a deeper understanding of hope; my thesis advisor, Dr. Deborah Sokolove (Wesley Theological Seminary), for believing in my thesis topic and helping me to write a scholarly paper; the Revd Rhonda Cooper, BCC (Johns Hopkins University Medical Center), for encouraging me to explore hope and suggesting resources for my literature review; Revd Sue Wintz, MDiv, BCC (Spiritual Care Association), who give me the opportunity to publish my writing on hope in PlainViews®; Chris Herman, LCSW-C, and Wendy Webb, LCSW-C, for offering suggestions to make the book accessible to a broader audience. Thanks go to all my Clinical Pastoral Education (CPE) supervisors who helped shape me into the chaplain I am today: the Revd Ellen Swinford (National Institutes of Health), the Revd Beth Godfrey and the Revd Donald Clem (Medstar Georgetown University Hospital), and Dr. Carol Battye (Johns Hopkins University Hospital-Bayview). Thanks also to Rabbi Gary Fink, DMin (Montgomery Hospice), for believing in me and suggesting the word "dimensions" of hope. I am so grateful for this word and believe it was the key to transforming the spirit of the book. And, most importantly, Linda J. MacNeil, who has given me unwavering support for the past 32 years. This book would not have been possible without her.

Introduction

I remember the exact moment in my life when I realized each of us will die someday. I was eight years old and alone in my bedroom watching the movie *West Side Story* on my small black-and-white television set. I wasn't prepared for what was about to happen. My mind began to race.

Tony was stabbed! Maria you have to help him! He's not moving. Maria is crying. What just happened? Did Tony die? How is that possible? He's too young. Only old people die. Grammy died when she was 92, and they wouldn't let me go to her funeral. I've never seen a dead person. Is Tony really dead? That makes no sense. He's not old. If Tony's dead, that means it could happen to anyone. That means my parents could die suddenly and leave me and my brother alone. Dad is much older than Mom. Oh no, he could die any minute!

I felt so scared and alone. I never told anyone about Tony. Instead I became obsessed with my father's death. Twenty-four years later, when my dad did die, I was rather surprised how well I handled it. I believe it all had to do with preparation. I had been preparing for his death for 24 years.

I think my obsession with death was a major factor in my decision to pursue a career in nursing. I wanted to help people postpone their death by helping to cure them and make them better. As I pursued my career in nursing, I soon found myself part of the medical system that refused to give up. We often performed cardio-pulmonary resuscitation (CPR) and placed patients on life support who had no chance of recovery. There was no such thing as a Do Not Resuscitate (DNR) order at the time. Later when a DNR order became a possible option, the medical team was reluctant to discuss it with the patient or family. I continued to witness many resuscitated people (who should have been given morphine to ease their pain and allowed to die peacefully) being held like Maria held Tony in the final scene of *West Side Story*.

I believe this futile escalation of care was a cause for many nurses to burn out and leave nursing all together. This is now recognized as moral distress (Austin, Saylor and Finlay 2017). My way of coping was to pursue additional education. I earned a Master's degree in primary care with a nurse practitioner certification, followed by a PhD in nursing ten years later. As a nurse practitioner, I continued to be part of a medical system that refused to give up no matter how dire the situation. Finding the next treatment became my framework for hope. Slowly I too burned out, finding refuge in a completely different line of work. For the last part of my career I worked as a project manager and then as a social scientist for the Food and Drug

Administration (FDA). It was a rewarding career move, but I missed working with patients and their families.

Not wanting to return to the stress of diagnosing and treating with limited time and personnel, I decided to follow my heart and pursue a career in spiritual care as a healthcare chaplain. Little did I know that becoming a chaplain would be one of the most challenging career moves I ever made. My first internship as a chaplain would later prove to be transformative.

Several weeks before retiring from the FDA and starting at the seminary, I met the young social scientist who was hired to replace me. Tragically, nine months later, she was diagnosed with an aggressive lymphoma. As fate would have it, she was admitted to the hospital unit I was assigned to as a new chaplain intern. I found our visits difficult as I witnessed her desperation to find the next clinical trial and her hope of getting a bone marrow transplant. The cancer was relentless. I found myself resenting the word "hope" and struggled to understand how to help her feel hopeful when there was little chance of finding another treatment option. I was at a loss as to how I could help and began questioning my career choice to become a healthcare chaplain. I knew that I needed to explore the concept of hope at the end-of-life, if I was going to continue down this new career path.

My exploration began in earnest during my second internship. This is when I realized that because I had been immersed in the medical model for over 30 years, the only hope I knew of was the hope of finding a cure. I had spent most of my nursing career working in a research environment where there always seemed to be another clinical trial—that was hope.

As I struggled to understand this better, I had a major breakthrough during a session with my spiritual director. At the time, I was writing the required theological reflection for my internship and had chosen to do my reflection on hope. As I described my former colleague's drive to find the next treatment, my spiritual director said that she seemed to be focused primarily on "hope that" another treatment would cure her disease and lacked "hope in," which is hope that arises from developing a sense of inner peace. Marilyn McEntyre describes "hoping in" as a theological virtue (McEntyre 2012, p.14). Immediately, I was able to conceptualize these two types of hope into real-life examples. I had seen many patients who only relied on the "hope that" a cure would be found. When they would reach the point when all medical options were exhausted, they often experienced great despair. The cancer patients I saw as a nurse practitioner were a perfect example. I also witnessed other patients who displayed a great deal of "hope in." These patients expressed disappointment in the lack of medical options, but they didn't seem to experience great despair. This is what I witnessed in many of the AIDS patients I took care of. They knew there was no cure, but somehow they managed to develop an amazing inner peace.

I believe that both types of hope are important. The conflict occurs when a person relies only on the "hope that" something or someone will make things better—this type of hope eventually runs out. Even Basil of Caesarea, an influential theologian in the early Christian church, realized this in the fourth century. According to Vigen Guroian, Professor of Religious Studies in Orthodox Christianity at the University of Virginia, Basil wrote that "rational or scientific medicine cannot save the human from death, but it can contribute to a healthy and meaningful life, so long as human beings do not put their whole hope in it" (Guroian in Lysaught and Ktova 2012, p.1074).

This framework became the core basis for my spiritual assessment. I found myself listening for "hope in" or "hope that" words or phrases during my conversations with patients. When I heard a patient say, "I know that no matter what happens I will be okay because I trust God," or "I know I will live forever through the love I have given to my children," I noted these as "hope in" statements. When I heard a patient say, "I'm not ready to give up, I know there is another treatment out there that will cure this cancer," or "I'm very hopeful that I will receive a transplant," I noted these as "hope that" statements. If I found a patient only speaking about "hope that," I would ask open-ended questions to look for "hope in" statements, such as, "You've been through a lot. What keeps you going? What gives you comfort? What gives you strength?"

Having an awareness of these two types of hope has changed the way I look at my own life. It has motivated me to cultivate my "hope in" by deepening my spiritual practice of contemplative prayer and meditation. I recognize the importance of cultivating "hope in" when things are going well. I have witnessed patients in spiritual crisis who never took the time to cultivate their "hope in" before they needed it. In turn, when all their options ran out, they were left feeling hopeless and in despair.

No one escapes death. Inevitably, each of us will come into contact with someone who is terminally ill. According to Elisabeth Kübler-Ross, hope is the one thing that usually persists through all the stages of death (Kübler-Ross 1969). Hope is complex. Without an understanding of its complexity, it is likely that spiritual care will fall short. Donald Capps, Professor of Pastoral Theology, believes that "the basic and fundamental role of the clergy is to be providers or agents of hope, and it is terribly difficult, if not impossible, to be an agent of hope if one has oneself lost hope" (Capps 1995, p.3). Therefore, I believe it is essential for a spiritual care provider to understand the complexity of hope and ways to cultivate hope when working with terminally ill patients and their families.

When I started as a chaplain intern, I would cringe at the word "hope," because I only saw hope in terms of medical options. With more experience, I began to feel comfortable with the concept of hope, but knew that I had only skimmed the surface and wanted to learn more. I chose to write my seminary thesis on hope at the end-of-life and, to my surprise, I discovered two more dimensions of hope in addition to "hope-in" and "hope-that."

The purpose of this book is to share what I discovered during my three-year exploration and to illustrate how these four dimensions of hope can be used as a framework for spiritual care. Chapter 1 is a review of the literature on hope at the end-of-life and how it has been described and categorized over the years. This chapter defines the four dimensions of hope and explains why it is beneficial to organize this information into these dimensions. Chapter 2 is an overview of the theology of hope and the role of a theological reflection in spiritual care. Chapter 3 explores ways to cultivate the four dimensions of hope, and the role of the chaplain. Chapter 4 provides case studies to demonstrate how the four dimensions of hope can be used as a framework for a spiritual assessment and for the development of a plan of care.

I hope you will find the information in this book useful as you journey alongside those who are facing death or as you prepare for your own mortality. We should all be cultivating the various dimensions of hope throughout our lives. Being prepared for our death gives us hope. Being unprepared for our death causes hopelessness and despair. Since we cannot escape death, we should at least do our best to prepare for it.

CHAPTER 1

The Concept of Hope

*The need to feel hopeful is part
of the human condition.*

According to the *Oxford Dictionary of English* (3rd edition)
hope is defined as: "A feeling of expectation and desire for a
particular thing to happen, a person or thing that may help
or save someone, grounds for believing something good may
happen and a feeling of trust."

Rabbi Maurice Lamm writes: "Like the bond in good paper,
hope is the watermark that is found in the very texture of the
human condition itself" (Lamm 1995, p.15).

The concept of hope emerged in the medical and
psychological literature in the 1950s (Eliott 2005). According
to Eliott (2005), Robin Downie, Emeritus Professor of Moral
Philosophy at the University of Glasgow, was one of the earliest
researchers to define hope in categories—*"hope that, hopeful
that, and hope to do"* (Downie 1963). These three categories

emphasized a person's process of hoping (Eliott 2005). A year later, psychoanalyst Erik Erikson saw hope as a human quality that changed over time influenced by "both spiritual and materialistic forces," with the most mature form of hope being that of faith which is not based on the need for evidence or reason (Eliott 2005, p.15). According to Capps, Erikson not only places "hope at the very beginning of the human life cycle but also considers hope to be the very heart and soul of the religious view of life and the world" (Capps 1995, p.6). In the same year, physician and scientist Abram Hoffer declared that "[t]he practice of medicine...had replaced hope" (Eliott 2005, p.15). The mature hope Erikson described, based purely on faith without evidence or reason, became hope in scientific discoveries. Medicine became the determinate of what hope is and what hope isn't (Eliott 2005). Christina M. Puchalski, M.D., director of the George Washington Institute of Spirituality, describes this as the source of hope being focused on "science and science's ability to cure illness and delay death. Healing became synonymous with cure" (Puchalski 2006, p.7). She adds, "Medical education focuses on our ability to diagnose, fix and cure, but until recently, little attention has been given to the concept of being present to another in the midst of their suffering and uncertainty" (Puchalski 2006, p.8).

According to Andrew Lester, Professor of Pastoral Theology, "hope or its absence, despair, is the basic psycho-spiritual dynamic with which the pastoral caregiver must contend, particularly when attending to a crisis" (Lester 1995, p.1). For most, the personal diagnosis of a terminal illness, or the terminal diagnosis of a loved one, is one of the most difficult crises one faces. Physician Elisabeth Kübler-Ross, in her seminal work based on her qualitative exploration of the stories shared by her dying patients, discovered that hope is the one thing that usually persists throughout the various stages of the dying process (Kübler-Ross 1969). The hope that she refers to in her well-known book *On Death and Dying* is classified as the hope for a cure. Based on her finding, Kübler-Ross believed it was important to maintain a person's hope for a cure even if a cure was not possible (Groopman 2004).

This type of hope that Bruce Rumbold, Professor of Pastoral Studies, calls "hope for recovery" (Rumbold 1986, p.60) is essentially the only type of hope the medical establishment has historically focused on. Much of this has to do with the ongoing assumption that by telling a patient they are dying, the patient "may become deeply depressed, even suicidal" (Rumbold 1986, p.13). In addition, there is often an overwhelming sense of helplessness experienced by the physician when they realize they are unable to provide a cure (Rumbold 1986). Megory Anderson in her book *Sacred Dying: Creating Rituals for Embracing the End of Life* contends that "most physicians tend to see death as the enemy; those who give in to it are the defeated victims. The doctor's role is to 'fix' a physical disorder, not to facilitate the transition between life and death" (Anderson 2003, p.17). According to Rumbold, helplessness is the number one cause of avoidance, and chaplains are not immune to this feeling. He notes: "Chaplains may practice a similar avoidance by retreating behind liturgy rather than risking a personal encounter with a dying patient" (Rumbold 1986, p.24). Christina Puchalski, in her book *A Time for Listening and Caring: Spirituality and the Care of the Chronically Ill and Dying*, writes, "I have worked with clergy who have avoided the topic [of death] for fear it was too depressing and would result in church members not returning to services" (Puchalski 2006, p.6). She adds that the reason for avoiding the topic of death has "more to do with our own basic discomfort with death" (Puchalski 2006, p.6). Rumbold and Kübler-Ross provided us with these key insights at a time when patients did not have legal access to their medical records. Rumbold emphasized that in order "for hope to emerge a person needs a realistic assessment of his situation" (Rumbold 1986, p.69). Thankfully, providing patients with full disclosure of their patient information upon request is now required by law. This has greatly facilitated the need for honest end-of-life discussions. However, as Jerome Groopman, M.D., describes in his book *The Anatomy of Hope: How People Prevail in the Face of Illness*, maintaining hope in patients, as well as admitting to a sense of helplessness, continues to be a struggle for many physicians. These challenging conversations are now being addressed in the medical literature. Rhonda Cooper, an oncology chaplain at Johns Hopkins University Hospital in Baltimore, Maryland, is working with colleagues to discover ways to help physicians improve communication with patients when they speak of faith and hope in light of a poor medical prognosis (Cooper *et al.* 2014). Conversations that center on the hope for a miracle can be especially difficult for most physicians. Groopman narrates how he came to understand the importance of maintaining hope for patients with terminal illness but not necessarily hope in the form of a miracle or cure. Groopman specifically cites his disagreement with Kübler-Ross's definition of hope (Groopman 2004) and refers to his finding "the middle ground where both truth and hope [can] reside" (p.57). Groopman summarizes this new understanding of hope as follows:

> *[T]he kind of hope she [the patient] showed me was very different from what Kübler-Ross described. Barbara's hope*

was real and undying. In her case it reflected the fact that she had found purpose and created meaning in her life through relationships with her loved ones, and with her God...she saw death as a natural part of life. It is not necessary to be a person of profound faith to hold this view and to act on it. (Groopman 2004, p.144)

By observing the impact of open and honest end-of-life discussions, Groopman, as well as others, have discovered that hope for a cure is not the only type of hope and that there are other types of hope that patients exhibit which are often influenced by "the touchstones of one's heritage and faith" (Groopman 2004, p.78). Groopman declares that there are two types of hope: "true hope" and "false hope." "False hope does not recognize the risks and dangers that true hope does. False hope can lead to intemperate choices and flawed decision making. True hope takes into account the real threats that exist and seek[s] to navigate the best path around them" (Groopman 2004, p.198). Groopman discovered that love and legacy are the universal foundation for true hope. "Uncertain of God, he looked to love and how it would shape the future of his family. Uncertain of an afterlife, he believed in the persistence of memory to make his presence palpable when he was gone" (Groopman 2004, p.145). Groopman also concludes, as Kübler-Ross did years earlier, that hope is essential. "Hope, then, is the ballast that keeps us steady, that recognizes where along the path are the dangers and pitfalls that can throw us off; hope tempers fear so we can recognize dangers and then bypass or endure them" (Groopman 2004, p.199). Groopman's memoir represents an important turning point in the medical field where hope is finally no longer placed in just one category, the hope for a cure.

As seen with Groopman, placing hope into categories is frequently done by those who write on this topic. Andrew Lester, who writes on hope in the context of pastoral care and the importance of understanding our future stories, places hope in two categories, which he calls "finite hope" and "transfinite hope" (Lester 1995, pp.63–4). Finite hope is hope that is temporary and transfinite hope is that which is not temporary. Examples of finite hope include "our hope in finite objects, desires and processes" (Lester 1995, p.63). Lester speaks of the importance of finite hope in terms of survival, such as finding food, employment, and safety. Transfinite hope is the ability to imagine an open-ended future as the basis for maintaining hope (Lester 1995, p.65). Lester stresses the necessity of transfinite hope in order to prevent despair: "When we have no horizon of open-ended future behind specific goals, we are vulnerable to despair" (Lester, 1995, p.67). Lester explains transfinite hope in Christian terms by citing Paul's letter to the Romans: "For in hope we were saved. Now hope that is seen is not hope. For who hopes for what is seen? But if we hope for what we do not see, we wait for it with patience" (Romans 8.24–5, NRSV). Capps characterizes this type of "patience" as "steadfastness, the ability to continue hope even as we are sorely tempted to give it up" (Capps 1995, p.150). The biblical passage in 1 Peter describes this as "the hope that is in you" (1 Peter 3.15, NRSV). Lester also describes an additional category of hope which the psychiatrist Karl Menninger refers to as "hope with" stressing that one goal of the pastoral relationship is to guide persons who express hopelessness in "developing meaningful relationships with a community of hopers" (Lester 1995, pp.98–9).

In the Book of Job, Job's friends recognized how to provide hope in the present moment: "They sat with him on the ground seven days and seven nights, and no one spoke a word to him, for they saw that his suffering was great" (Job 2.13). Once they opened their mouths they were no longer present with him. They shifted to looking at the past, trying to determine what Job had done wrong to cause his terrible affliction in an attempt to understand his future. They no longer journeyed with him in the present moment.

The Protestant German theologian Jürgen Moltmann explains that when hope is conceived as something that is future-oriented we actually cheat ourselves from having hope:

> *We do not rest satisfied with the present. We anticipate the future as too slow in coming, as if in order to hasten its course; or we recall the past, to stop its too rapid flight. So imprudent are we that we wander in times which are not ours, and do not think of the only one which belongs to us; and so idle are we that we dream of those times which are not more, and thoughtlessly overlook that which alone exists... We scarcely ever think of the present; and if we think of it, it is only to take light from it to arrange the future. (Moltmann 1967, p.26)*

In other words, hope is found in the present moment. This concept of hope in the present moment is also described by the twentieth-century theologian Paul Tillich, who suggests that people who lose sight of the present moment are not able to enter into Divine rest: "They are held to the past and cannot separate themselves from it, or they escape towards the future, unable to rest in the present. They have not entered the eternal rest which stops the flux of time and gives us the blessing of the present" (Tillich 1956, p.131).

Capps also stresses the importance of appreciating the present moment:

> *Another risk that hope presents is that we become so oriented toward the attainment [of a future situation] that we neglect the satisfactions our present situation already affords...when we experience satisfaction in our present reality, we allow love an equally significant place in our lives." (Capps 1995, p.76)*

Kaethe Weingarten, a psychologist and writer who writes about her struggle with a life-threatening illness, describes hope in the present moment as "reasonable hope—what is possible right now—even in the face of severe illness." She further states that reasonable hope "offers a platform on which to stand even when you cannot bear what you must carry." Reasonable hope "calls you back to the present moment...[and] will help you thrive in the face of uncertainty" (Weingarten, quoted in Willis 2013, pp.57–8).

Kathleen Singh, in her book *The Grace in Dying: A Message of Hope, Comfort, and Spiritual Transformation*, recounts various stages of dying, with the final stage being that of surrender. Prior to this stage there is a period of chaos which includes denial, anger, bargaining, depression, and acceptance (Singh 1982). She writes: "The stage of acceptance is the acknowledgement that the sand is passing through the hourglass and the remaining grains are few...[and] the mental ego has accepted the fact of its impeding demise. (Singh 1982, p.193). She says, "Acceptance is dying while living...[the final stage] surrender, is living while dying" (Singh 1982, pp.196–7). She notes that it is at this stage that a person experiences pure awareness of self, liberated from the consciousness of the ego, and also writes, "Surrender is not giving up...surrender is entering the moment... Attention shifts to Reality, to Life itself" (Singh 1982, pp.226, 237). She further describes how "When hope evaporates, we are left with the here and now. Hope, a posture of the mental ego, is transformed into presence, a stance of the Spirit" (Singh 1982, p.96). Stephen Levine asserts in his book *Who Dies? An Investigation of Conscious Living and Conscious Dying* that "there is no other preparation for death except opening to the present" (Levine 1982, p.33). Leonard Jacobson, a spiritual writer, describes the stage of surrender as "a silent knowing that you are in God and God is in you, and that you and God are One" (Jacobson 2007, p.185). The stage of surrender is hope in the present moment.

Summary

The need to feel hopeful is part of the human condition. As seen from this review of the literature, defining hope can be difficult and complex because hope can change and evolve over time. Hope can be described as the opposite of despair; however, cultivating only one type of hope may lead to despair. When hope is a solitary belief that someone or something will fix an unchangeable circumstance, it can become the absence of light. But when hope is an undercurrent empowering a person to surrender and trust, it can become a beacon of light.

Often spiritual care providers instinctively understand the tremendous power of hope but may find it difficult to conceptualize it and place it in a framework for patient care. After reviewing the literature on the concept of hope in spiritual care, I propose categorizing this information into four dimensions: *Hope-that, Hope-in, Hope-with* and *Hope-in-the-present-moment*. Each of these dimensions is defined as follows:

- *Hope-that* is the hope which is external, dependent on something outside of ourselves. It is a hope that relies on the workings of another person or the creation of something that will fix or change a situation. It is the hope that medicine will find a cure for a disease. It is the hope that the police will find a missing child. It is the hope that a new device will help improve a person's life. It is the hope that comes with knowing one's affairs are in order, loved ones will be cared for, and arrangements have been made to ensure a peaceful death.

- *Hope-in* is internal hope that comes from deep within and is not dependent on another person or material thing. It is a deep sense of a power greater than oneself, the meaning of one's life, the strong and reassuring sense of eternity through a belief in a Higher Power, the love passed onto others, or one's legacy. *Hope-in* is a feeling that may be difficult to describe. It is often a sense of peace and serenity that comes from believing that there is something more beyond this life. *Hope-in* allows one to trust and to surrender; to recognize that not everything is in our control.

- *Hope-with* is the hope that comes from having connectivity with other people. It is the hope that grows out of support and a sense of not being alone, no matter how difficult the situation. It is a sense of peace that comes with having a medical team who will always be there even if they no longer have a treatment. It is the hope that allows a person to let go and deeply trust in the care given to them by other people. It is also the hope that comes after reconciliation with loved ones who had become separated from a person's life.

- *Hope-in-the-present-moment* is the hope that comes from understanding what it means to be mindful. It is a sense of peace in knowing the only moment that can be counted on is the present moment. It is the hope that comes with the ability to surrender to the moment. It allows one to let go of any worries from the past or fears about the future. This is the most important hope we can cultivate because the present moment is the only moment that is guaranteed.

These four dimensions of hope may be experienced differently for each individual. Some people may only experience one type of hope while others may find all of them to be relevant. Alternatively, someone in great despair may have no hope at all. Rumbold reminds us that we need to compassionately meet a person where they are without judgment because ultimately there is no right or wrong experience.

[T]here are individuals who will insist upon denial right to the end; others will fight—literally—until their last breath. Neither approach is very satisfactory; but it may be thoroughly appropriate to the dying person's life. And for me to say that it is not satisfactory of course reveals something of what I think dying ought to be like. (Rumbold 1986, p.88)

The dimension of hope that one experiences will most likely evolve over time. *Hope-that* a cure will be found may or may not transition to a *Hope-that* a peaceful death will occur. *Hope-in* knowing there is something beyond medicine, something greater than oneself, something eternal, may be experienced by some people early in their end-of-life journey. For others, it may need to be cultivated or it may never occur at all. *Hope-with* that is experienced through personal relationships may also need to be cultivated through reconciliation or the ability to reach out and seek help. And finally, for most people, finding *Hope-in-the-present-moment* may be their greatest struggle. Spiritual guidance is often needed to cultivate this type of hope. One way is to simply listen and be fully present. By doing this, the spiritual care provider becomes an exemplar of *Hope-in-the-present-moment*. To be fully present in the moment with another person, and meeting them in whatever dimension of hope they may be experiencing, is the very core of spiritual care. As Steve Nolan discovered, one of the most important roles of a chaplain is to be a "hopeful presence" (Nolan 2012, p.127).

CHAPTER 2

The Theology of Hope

*A significant role of the chaplain is to
help a person discover hope that is greater
than the limitations of medicine.*

Of all the dimensions of hope, the *Hope-in* dimension is the most complex. For this reason, I have decided to dedicate an entire chapter on this one dimension. As with all encounters, it is always important to meet people where they are in their spiritual journey. For the dying patient, a significant role of the chaplain is to help them shift from solely focusing on *Hope-that* a cure will be found to also focusing on *Hope-in* something greater than the limitations of medicine. If a person is open to making such a shift, they can begin to explore hope that comes from deep within. Capps defines this as shifting from "hopes related to our present life on earth to hopes concerning the life to come" (Capps, 1995, p.72). Capps further expounds that:

Most of us have the desire that death will not be final, and whatever form our existence may take after we die, it will be more whole and complete than our earthly life has been. We have this desire, but we differ a great deal in our anticipation that this will in fact occur. For some of us, our anticipation of such an afterlife is very strong. For others, it is rather weak. Its strength or weakness is influenced by many factors but is related in part to where we have found a way to image our future beyond the grave. (Capps 1995, pp.72–3)

According to the most recent Pew Research Center poll, 97% of Americans report believing in a Higher Power, and of these, 76.5% affiliate with a particular faith, while 20.5% declare themselves non-affiliated; a significant number of those who report believing in a Higher Power believe there is a heaven (72%) and a hell (58%) (Ritchey 2015). How one recognizes a Higher Power in their life and their concepts of heaven and hell, varies considerably. According to Andrew Lester, Professor of Pastoral Theology, we are temporal beings; therefore we understand everything in the context of past, present, and future. Lester emphasizes that we all have a perception of what we think will happen in our future, which we construct as our future stories. Our future stories shape our perception of hope and our ability to hope makes us human (Lester 1995). He underscores the fact that we perceive our future stories based on what has happened to us in our past. Hope occurs in the present in that we actively hope, however it is based on our understanding of the past, and it "receives its energy from the future" (Lester 1995, p.15). Lester urges spiritual care providers not to overlook a person's future story. It is important to understand one's perceptions of their past and present but he believes that asking a person about their future is equally important and often overlooked. "We can offer quality care to any individual, group, or system only if we know their future stories as well as their past and present stories" (Lester 1995, p.41).

Since it is essential to listen to a person's future story, one may simply ask a person, "Tell me some stories about your future?" (Lester 1995, p.55). One may assess whether or not their story seems realistic based on the situation. Lester points out that "hope based on distortions...turns out to be false hope that leads to hopelessness" (Lester 1995, p.86). Is the person fearful or hesitant to describe their future? Being fearful of something that will occur in the future that involves loss is often referred to as "anticipatory grief." Lester illustrates the importance of inviting a person "to conceptualize how life will be different in the future if or when the loss occurs...and enabling the grieving person to slowly reframe a future story in which the lost person or object is eased out of the picture" (Lester 1995, p.51). This process of conceptualization helps a person shift from a feeling of hopelessness and despair to a feeling of hope. When describing the future story of the dying, Lester refers to this as their sacred story. "[E]veryone has a sacred story that includes his or her ultimate belief about the future" (Lester 1995, p.93).

One cannot assume to know a person's sacred story. Anderson describes the importance of asking a dying person about their concept of an afterlife as a way to understand their sacred story. She emphasizes that this is especially important with children, because children often "have wonderful images of what the next life will be" (Anderson 2003, p.23). Listening to their child's belief in what is going to happen can be extremely helpful for parents as they deal with this difficult situation (Anderson 2003).

It is important to note that a sacred story is not always one that provides comfort; for example, a person whose God of their knowing is one of judgment and condemnation may cause them to be very fearful of their future (Lester 1995). This can even result in a person feeling undeserving of hope (Groopman 2004). When God is "related to law rather than grace...[t]he hope that was potentially theirs has been short circuited by what they have learned about the nature and character of this God and how this God relates to humans" (Lester 1995, p.82). On the contrary, a recent study found that individuals who believe in a benevolent God feel more grateful to God and, in turn, feel more hopeful. This study also concluded that a greater sense of hope is associated with greater health (Krause, Emmons and Ironson 2015). Lester stresses the importance of listening to a person's sacred story and, while maintaining respect for their beliefs, gently reframing their judgmental God into a benevolent God when appropriate (Lester 1995, p.93).

Carrie Doehring, in her book *The Practice of Pastoral Care: A Postmodern Approach*, delineates this process as shifting from an embedded theology to a deliberative theology. "When a person becomes aware of their embedded theology in the midst of a crisis, they often go through a process of evaluating their beliefs and reconstructing new ones. As they do this they are engaging in deliberative theology" (Doehring 2006, p.112). Puchalski describes this process as follows:

Spiritual journeys can be shaped and challenged by the facing of uncertainty and mystery. Previous beliefs, such as the universality of God's power, the belief that prayer brings cures, that one's community can help overcome all suffering, or that science has all the answers, might not be of help in the face of inevitable death...people may give up entirely on their beliefs

or may be spurred to evaluate their beliefs at a deeper level.
(Puchalski 2006, p.57)

Doehring (2006) says that embedded theologies develop over time outside of a person's conscious awareness and are generally based on the teachings and beliefs of their religious tradition, which often begins in childhood. She says that deliberative theologies, on the other hand, are actively constructed and often triggered when someone needs to make sense of suffering. She notes that this is when many things are sorted out by unpacking memories and appraising beliefs, feelings, values, and hopes—therefore, how a person perceives hope when faced with the crisis of a terminal illness has everything to do with their deliberative theology. She further notes that his can be a delicate balance, whereby a person attempts to conserve their embedded theology and, at the same time, reconstruct their embedded theology as it applies to what is currently happening in their life. According to Doehring (2006), the role of a spiritual care provider is to help guide a person as they embark on reconstructing their embedded theology.

Howard Stone and James Duke (2013) refer to this process of reconstructing one's theology as a theological reflection. Vital to this process is an assessment of the individual's embedded theological beliefs; for example, "are they life-giving or destructive at this moment of crisis?" (Doehring 2006, p.116). Doehring stresses the importance of drawing upon one's theological education in the process of "co-constructing a deliberative theology with the careseeker" (Doehring 2006, p.117). Bishop John Shelby Spong describes it this way: "[We] must arrive at the truth we seek by way of the religious system of our origins, not by rejecting or denying that system, but by transforming it" (Spong 2009, p.172). One example of this type of theological transformation can be found in Michael Morwood (2013) book, *It's Time: Challenges to the Doctrine of the Faith*.

As noted earlier in this chapter, hope is influenced by our perception of our future story. For someone confronting a terminal illness, their future story is generally shaped by their concept of an afterlife based on an emerging deliberative theology as they seek to make sense of their mortality. Determining how much of a person's deliberative theology is based on their embedded theology can be difficult. It is important to stress that it is not always necessary to understand a person's embedded theology unless the person's emerging deliberative theology appears to be destructive rather than positive and therapeutic.

Exploring an individual's theology of hope

When working with patients and their families, one of the first things a spiritual care provider tends to seek is information about their faith tradition. Although this is often found in the demographic information in the medical record, it is sometimes recorded incorrectly and does not provide information on their current practices and beliefs. As Anderson (2003) pointed out, the key to understanding *Hope-in* comes with exploring afterlife beliefs.

For the spiritual care provider, having a basic understanding of the afterlife beliefs within various faith traditions can be beneficial. Knowing the basic concepts can provide a foundation for assessing possible misconceptions and help alleviate misunderstandings. The following is a brief overview of the most common afterlife theological concepts. Ultimately, it is recommended to consult with a religious leader from a particular faith tradition if clarity is needed.

A brief survey of common afterlife theological concepts

One thing is certain, theological thinking continues to evolve as embedded theologies are reconstructed in response to current thinking. Stone and Duke point this out in their book *How to Think Theologically*: "[W]hat people understand their Christian faith to mean varies from one age to another, from denomination to denomination, from congregation to congregation and from person to person" (Stone and Duke 2013, p.14). Variations in deliberative theology can be as minor as scriptural interpretations by a church leader to a major shift with broad impact, such as the changing views on organ donation, female ordination, and homosexuality. The same is true for the theology of the afterlife. Since entire text books have been written on this topic, this chapter will only provide a brief survey of afterlife beliefs found in Christianity, Judaism, Islam, Hinduism, and Buddhism.

The concept of hope in the afterlife is based on what a person believes will happen to them after death. The Abrahamic traditions of Judaism, Christianity, and Islam share similar beliefs that focus on a new world that is yet to come. This is referred to as an "eschatological theology" or what one believes will happen at the end of time (the end of time being a separate event in the future, not the end of time of the individual at the moment of death). The Eastern traditions of Hinduism and Buddhism believe that the end of time is the point whereby a person finally achieves complete union with all that is in the universe, thus freeing them from the cycle of death and rebirth (Hick 1994). The Eastern concept of complete universal unification is also found in the deliberative theologies of Judaism, Christianity, and Islam, especially within the mystic traditions (McColman 2010).

Afterlife in Christianity

The Christian concept of the afterlife is as varied as the tradition itself. The traditional Christian view of the afterlife is based on the resurrection of Jesus, the Parousia or second coming of Christ, and the eschaton or end of times and the Day of Judgment. Twenty-first-century theologian Jürgen Moltmann (1967) renders the traditional view that the resurrection of Christ is the theological foundation of Christian hope in his book *Theology of Hope*. However, his concept of eschatology or end of times deviates somewhat from traditional thinking, which tends to be entirely based on a future event when there will be the violent end of the world followed by the establishment of God's kingdom (Segal 2004). Moltmann argues that the term "eschatology" is wrong. According to him, there is no end of time because it is "the promise of the coming of God" (Moltmann 1975, p.45). He sees hope as a current as well as a future process and criticizes the fact that Christian theology has placed too much emphasis on a future event. This is not unlike Marcus Borg, another twenty-first-century theologian, who describes the second coming as:

> *[T]he return of Jesus already experienced as the risen Christ and the Spirit of Christ. It is Jesus coming again in the rhythms of the Christian liturgical year. Advent is preparing for the coming of Jesus—about the coming of Christ who is already here... And what is meant by the second coming is also the*

ultimate Christian hope—for that time...when "God will be all in all" (1 Cor. 15:28). (Borg 2011, p.195)

Fr. Richard Rohr, a Franciscan priest and spiritual leader, describes the second coming of Christ in a similar way:

> *Henceforth, the Christ "comes again" whenever we are able to see the spiritual and the material coexisting, in any moment, in any event, and in any person. All matter reveals Spirit, and Spirit needs matter to "show itself." I believe "the Second Coming of Christ" happens whenever and wherever we allow this to be utterly true for us. This is how God continually breaks into history—even before the first Stone Age, humans stood in awe and wonder, gazing at the stars. (Rohr 2016)*

The concept of what happens to the dead during the "intermediate time," or that time before Christ's return, has evolved over the centuries. In the first century, Christians believed that Christ's return and the end of this world was imminent (Sumegi 2014). As time passed, concern arose over what happens to the "soul" after death as it waits for the second coming of Christ. As a result, further development of the concept of heaven and hell emerged and later evolved to include purgatory, an in-between realm where purification takes place (Sumegi 2014). The concept of heaven and hell remains within most mainline Christian traditions, as well as some other faith traditions. The concept of purgatory continues to remain within the Catholic tradition (Sumegi 2014). However, the deliberative theology of Moltmann and others have moved away from heaven, hell, and purgatory in the literal sense—instead there is a growing emphasis on different states of the soul being in relationship with God (Sumegi 2014).

The belief that afterlife would entail the resurrection of the physical body has been debated for thousands of years (Sumegi 2014). Most non-orthodox Christian traditions have evolved in their concept of physical bodily resurrection as evidenced by the current thinking regarding organ transplantation (Finger Lakes Donor Recovery Network (2016). However, according to some traditional Christians, the time when death will be no more is yet to come and will occur when Christ returns. This is the time when the spirit will be in full relationship with God (Moltmann 1977). In the meantime, the spirit or soul exists in an intermediate time.

What happens to the soul during this time as it awaits an eternal relationship with God? Some theologians believe that the soul continues to develop. This belief is expressed by Moltmann and John Hick, a twenty-first-century theologian. Moltmann believes that God created us all as unique beings who will continue to develop after death. According to Moltmann, this is especially important for those who have an untimely death (Moltmann 1977).

Hick describes a similar belief that none of us completely develop into the person God intends us to be in our lifetime. According to Hick, our souls continue to develop after death, which he refers to as "soul making." He writes that "soul making" begins in this life and continues after our bodily death (Hick 2010, pp.333–6). As Hick puts it, the meaning of our lives is fulfilled in the future after our death according to "God's purpose" (Hick 2010, p.48). We grow as free beings towards a fullness of personal life "in conscious relationship to God, which represents the Divine purpose for us" (Hick 2010, p.49). Hick believes that we eventually move past our ego-selves to a higher unity which cannot be achieved in our lifetime; therefore, our souls will continue to develop to achieve this unity after death (Hick 2010).

Others consider what happens to us after death to be a mystery; for example, "It will be a transformation into another way of living on in the ultimate mystery—a way beyond all our thoughts and images, a way beyond our human knowing" (Morwood 2007, p.201).

Afterlife in Judaism

As with Christianity, there is a vast array of deliberative theologies within the other faith traditions regarding the afterlife. The concept of afterlife in Judaism has also evolved significantly and differs within the practices of Orthodox, Conservative, Reform, and Reconstructionist Judaism. Judaism places far less emphasis on the afterlife than Christianity (Segal 2004). Rabbi Maurice Lamm reports that the reason for this is because "[t]he Bible, so vitally concerned with the actions of man in this world, and agonizing over day-to-day morals, is relatively silent about the world-to-come" (Lamm 1969, pp.221–2).

The earliest biblical concept of the afterlife was a place called Sheol. The dominant thinking was that all people eventually end up in Sheol in some combination of body and spirit and this is where they stayed forever (Goldenberg 1992). Later Jewish thinking, possibly influenced by the Greeks or Persians, shifted to thinking of the body and soul as separate entities (Goldenberg 1992). The body was seen as "a corrupt prison from which the pure spirit or soul longed to be free, [and therefore death] was seen as a kind of liberation" (Goldenberg 1992, p.100). Although one group of Jewish leaders, the Sadducees, continued to oppose concepts of the afterlife, the Pharisees "expected a resurrection of the dead in the Days of the Messiah" (Borowitz 1984, p.214). The Days of the Messiah was understood as the day when an ideal king will come and "reestablish Jewish rule in the Holy Land, gather in the Jewish exiles, and inaugurate a perfect society, starting with humankind toward the life of the world-to-come" (Borowitz 1984, p.77). The Pharisees believed that:

> *God takes our souls when we die, and they enter a period of purifying punishment... God then returns our souls to a heavenly 'treasury' where they await the earthly coming of the Messiah. Sometime after that event, the graves are opened and the bodies, made perfect and pure, arise from them. The souls are restored to them, completing the resurrection of the dead ...the revived person then comes before God for final judgment. The righteous go straight into the life of the world-to-come...the wicked are punished until they are purified and permitted entry into the world-to-come or else are doomed to destruction and denied the bliss of eternal life. (Borowitz 1984, pp.214–15)*

The concept of hell is known as *Gehinnom* (Segal 2004).

This Pharisaic concept dominated as persecution increased (Sumegi 2014) and is the doctrine of afterlife that continues to this day in traditional Judaism (Borowitz 1984) although different views have emerged over the centuries, including the belief in the pre-existence of souls and reincarnation among those who follow the way of Kabbalah, an ancient Jewish mystical tradition (Sumegi 2014).

There are also different views concerning the body. Positive views of the body require that the body be restored after death, and negative views of the body require only the "spirit, or soul, or mind be liberated from its material prison to enjoy its proper reward" (Goldenberg 1992, p.106). The concept of bodily resurrection is held by traditional Jews because "Judaism has always stressed that the body, as the soul, is a gift from God, that it belongs to God" (Lamm 1969, p.232). There are also those who have held the belief that the spirit survives after death whereupon it is reunited with God (Borowitz 1984). According to Rabbi Borowitz, a modern twenty-first-century Jew, most Jews today have given up a belief in an afterlife (Borowitz 1984) and they no longer believe in the coming of a messianic figure who will "bring the world complete justice, peace, and well-being" (Borowitz 1984, p.77). Instead "they emphasize the good that people need to do while they are alive" (Borowitz 1984, p.219) and they believe in the coming of a Messianic Age "whereby humankind works together to create a perfect world" (Borowitz 1984, p.82). To many modern Jews, the concept of afterlife is the ability to "pass on a loving memory of their deceased from generation to generation" (Kertzer 1993, p.84). This is why legacy, life review, and saying the Kaddish in memory of deceased family members are so important. It is also important to note that some Jews do not have religious beliefs but still identify themselves as being Jewish based on their cultural origins.

Afterlife in Islam

The Islamic concept of afterlife has also evolved over time. The basic Islamic concepts of reward and punishment are similar to the traditional concepts found in Christianity and Judaism. For "the person who chooses to turn away from God…the time will come when he or she must account for that choice and receive God's judgement" (Sumegi 2014, p.137). Islam accepts the idea of life after death in which the person survives in some type of form or essence and will be "reunited with the body at the time of resurrection to receive God's judgement" (Sumegi 2014, p.143). According to Islamic belief, the non-physical aspect of the person consists of the soul (*nafs*) and the breath of life or Divine spirit (*ruh*). The *nafs* is "the ethical character of a person, the aspect which pertains to rationality and intelligence that can develop in noble ways that can change and grow toward God or away from God" (Sumegi 2014, p.143).

There is a variety of deliberative theological views based on scriptural interpretation as to whether or not the *nafs*, the *ruh*, or both survive after death (Sumegi 2014), although:

> [T]here is general agreement that resurrection and life after death pertain to individual identity, and that there is some aspect of one's identity that will experience the events that take place between death and resurrection whether pleasurable or painful. (Sumegi 2014, p.146)

The Quran speaks of a Day of Judgment in which the dead will be given the reward of paradise or the punishment of hell (Sumegi 2014). Before the Day of Judgment and resurrection to either paradise or hell "the soul exists in an intermediate place and state called *barzakh* [where the soul] receives punishment or reward according to its former deeds" (Sumegi 2014, p.148). A person is questioned by the angel of death (*Izra'il*) during their first night in the grave. Answers to the questions "Who is your Lord?" (*Allah*) and "Who is your prophet?" (*Mohammed*), in addition to the number of good deeds accomplished, determine if the intermediate time spent before resurrection will be pleasant or unpleasant (Sumegi 2014). Later Islamic authorities describe this as a time when "the soul undergoes constant growth and transformation on the basis of the deeds it performed in the world" (Chittick 1992, p.137). The Day of Judgment is a time only known to God. It is believed that it will be "a cataclysmic destruction of the entire universe" (Sumegi 2014, p.150). At this time, all will be gathered for judgment, with each person being brought before God where the destiny of paradise or hell for the resurrected will be determined (Sumegi 2014). Islamic interpretation of what will happen on the Day of Judgment also varies significantly. Traditional Islamic teachings speak of a permanent hell (Chittick 1992, p.137), whereas modern Islamic teachings speak of hell as a place of purification. A place where "[the soul] may be awakened to the higher life…[because] the purpose of God must be ultimately fulfilled and, though man may bring down punishment on himself by his deeds, yet as God has created him for mercy, mercy is the ultimate end in the Divine scheme" (Ali 2002, pp.49–50). In other words, "God's all-embracing and precedent mercy gives solace even to the damned" (Chittick 1992, p.138).

Afterlife in Hinduism and Buddhism

Hinduism and Buddhism are spiritual traditions based on the belief that intentional actions (*karma*) influence the cycle of death and rebirth (*samsara*) (Sumegi 2014). The Buddha was a Hindu who "rejected the [Hindu] orthodox belief of his time that the eternal soul (*atman*) transmigrated from life to life taking on new forms until it achieved final liberation" (Sumegi 2014, p.204). Buddha believed that "the human personality is without a soul or unchanging essence" (Sumegi 2014, p.196). For both Hinduism and Buddhism, the aim is to eventually break the cycle of death and rebirth (*moksha*) and achieve the final state. The Hindu understanding of the final state is the "total absorption into the Infinite Consciousness, the larger stream of thought...[with a] continuing identity in which the soul is both somehow part of the life of God and yet somehow still exists in personal relationship of love of God" (Hick 1994, p.431). Many Buddhist groups do not believe in God or gods. Their understanding of the final state following liberation or *moksha* is called *pari-nirvana*, which is "the final and complete ending of individual selfhood in the infinite and eternal Reality" (Hick 1994, p.436) The Buddhist believe this state of *nirvana* or enlightenment, which Buddha achieved, can also be attained in this life, although it is an indescribable experience that only few are able to attain (Hick 1994). In essence, the theology of hope for both Hindus and Buddhists is to base one's actions (*karma*) on the goal of eventually breaking the cycle of death and rebirth (*moksha*), thereby attaining the final state of perfect union with eternal reality.

Summary

When providing spiritual care to the dying, it is important to gain insight into a person's future story. What do they believe will happen to them after they die? This invites an understanding of a person's theology and their internal hope or *Hope-in*.

A person's concept of afterlife is most often related to their beliefs associated with a particular faith tradition. However, it's important to note that spiritual care providers also work with people who do not have a faith tradition or do not believe in a Higher Power. Recently, spirituality and religion have been separated into distinct constructs (Steinhauser *et al.* 2017) whereby spirituality is defined "more broadly encompassing the search for the "significant," "sacred," or that which holds ultimate meaning or purpose (e.g., relationships with others, the transcendent, nature or the self)" (McSherry and Cash 2004). According to Puchalski, "[o]ne can have specific spiritual beliefs, rituals, and practices, or not. Spirituality does not imply any belief in a supreme being. Religion refers to beliefs, practices, and rituals within the context of a specific system of beliefs" (Puchalski 2006, p.10). Puchalski further cites a survey conducted on dying patients in 1997 by the George H. Gallup International Institute. The predominant response to the question asking what brings a person comfort was the "need to believe that death is a normal part of the life cycle and they would live on through their relationships, their accomplishments and good works" (Puchalski 2006, p.13). This desire to find meaning in one's life is universal and it is the role of the spiritual care provider to assist in this search for meaning.

For the dying who do have religious beliefs, their beliefs are based on a deliberative theology which evolves over time. A person's deliberative theology is most often founded on their embedded theology, which developed in their childhood or when they were first exposed to a particular faith tradition. As an interfaith chaplain I have come to realize that it is more important to understand a person's developing deliberative theology than it is to have an in-depth understanding of their embedded theology. As we minister to the suffering, the "task requires attention not to the fine points of theological doctrine but to the reality of the patient's experience of pain and our certainty of God's love" (Mohrmann 2012, p.467).

As we journey beside someone who is reconstructing their theology in response to a crisis, we should ask ourselves the following question: Do their beliefs provide them with a sense of safety, peace and comfort or a sense of anxiety, sadness and fear? Put simply, do their beliefs provide them with hope or leave them feeling hopeless and in despair? If the answer is hopelessness and despair, the next step is to ask ourselves how we can guide them to reconstruct their emerging deliberative theology into a theology of hope. Sometimes it can be as simple as giving a person permission to think of God in another way. Giving someone permission to change their theology can be transformative. I believe the following is one of the best examples of *Hope in* arising from reconstructing an embedded theology into a deliberative theology in a time of crisis.

In 1935 the first edition of *The Big Book* for Alcoholics Anonymous (AA) was printed. The first chapter, entitled "Bill's Story," is the story of the founder of AA. He narrates that his life was in ruins due to his alcohol abuse. He had reached rock-bottom when his life suddenly changed. A friend came to visit who was also an alcoholic but now sober. Bill was shocked. His friend seemed like a different person. When Bill asked him how he did it, his friend responded, "I've got religion" (Alcoholics Anonymous 1935, p.10). Bill thought his friend had lost his mind. As his friend continued to talk, Bill described memories of his faith tradition:

> *Childhood memories rose before me. I could almost hear the sound of the preacher-voice as I sat, on still Sunday's, way over there on the hillside ...[and then] there was my grandfather's good natured contempt of some church folk and their doings... and the denial of the preacher's right to tell him how he must listen...these recollections welled up from the past. They made me swallow hard. (Alcoholics Anonymous 1935, p.10)*

Bill then grapples with what he believes:

> *[I believe in a] power greater than myself...[but] with ministers, and world's religions, I parted right there...I became irritated and my mind snapped shut against such a theory...the wars which had been fought, the burnings and chicanery that religious dispute had facilitated, made me sick. (Alcoholics Anonymous 1935, pp.10–11)*

His friend affirmed that what God had done for him, he could not have done for himself. This caused Bill to begin reconstructing his embedded theology into a deliberative theology:

> *Never mind the musty past; here sat a miracle directly across the kitchen table...[however] the word God still aroused a certain antipathy. When the thought was expressed that there might be a God personal to me this feeling was intensified. I didn't like the idea. I could go for such conceptions as Creative Intelligence, Universal Mind or Spirit of Nature but resisted the thought of a Czar of the Heavens, however loving His sway might be. (Alcoholics Anonymous 1935, p.12)*

Then his friend suggested, "*Why don't you choose your own conception of God?*" (Alcoholics Anonymous 1935, p.12). Bill's response represents his transformation from despair to hope:

> *That statement hit me hard. It melted the icy intellectual mountain in whose shadow I had lived and shivered for many years. I stood in the sunlight at last...scales of pride and prejudice fell from my eyes. A new world came to view. (Alcoholics Anonymous 1935, p.12)*

Bill discovered *Hope-in* through his friend who gave him permission to think of God in another way, not based on a dogma that he was taught. I believe that as a chaplain this is one of the best gifts we can offer. It is the gift of freedom to discover the God of our knowing and the impact this has on our *Hope-in,* as well as our future stories of life after death.

CHAPTER 3

Cultivating Hope

*Discovering ways to help cultivate hope at
the end-of-life requires an open heart and
the ability to let go and allow the Spirit
to work through you in the moment.*

I believe one of the most important roles of the chaplain is to guide people to explore new ways to understand and experience hope by being a steady companion in the present moment. This is what Steve Nolan describes as "being with" (Nolan 2012, p.110). According to the spiritual writer Leonard Jacobson, "awaken from the past and future into the present and you become a vehicle for God. You are actively bringing Heaven to Earth" (Jacobson 2015, p.96). Discovering ways to help cultivate hope at the end-of-life requires an open heart and the ability to let go and allow the Spirit to work through you in the moment. In doing so, the opportunities are endless and often filled with unexpected surprises.

The following is a survey of some modalities that can be utilized to cultivate hope at the end-of-life. There is no right or wrong way to foster these modalities. It is only important to trust, allow your creativity to flow, and let the Spirit guide you.

Storytelling, journaling, letter-writing, and poetry

Robert McDowell writes, 'Through poetry, we gain greater self-understanding as well as insight into others in our world and into our world itself' (McDowell 2008, p.2). It is essential for chaplains, through empathetic and reflective listening, to "learn about the disease in the context of the patient's story, his or her beliefs, values, relationships, hopes, fears, and dreams" (Puchalski 2006, p.21). Kathleen Dowling Singh notes that most people who are facing the reality of the end of their life conduct a life review as a way to process what is happening until "what is inessential begins to evaporate, disappearing like dew in the morning" (Singh 1982, p.202). Therefore, storytelling is not only an important step in letting go of the past and future in order to experience *Hope-in-the-present-moment*, it also fosters *Hope-with* and *Hope-in*. Storytelling creates a means to intimately connect with others while leaving one's legacy, which can contribute to a sense of immortality. Storytelling also allows for an important life review and meaning-making. Puchalski points out that "as people review their lives, they may reframe past experiences in a different way in order to give a new and more significant meaning to their lives" (Puchalski 2006, p.78) Additionally, "interventions that focus on increasing or maintaining a sense of meaning and purpose...may have substantial impact in reducing one's sense of hopelessness" (Puchalski 2006, p.274).

Through storytelling, a person may be able to shift from a focus on the *Hope-that* a cure will be found, to *Hope-that* they will experience a peaceful death. Anderson makes a similar declaration: "We cannot 'fix' death as modern medicine wants us to believe; we can only attempt to help our loved ones make the dying transition a peaceful one" (Anderson 2003, p.21). Singh characterizes storytelling as an opportunity for closure: "It is a step in the movement beyond the mental ego, in preparation for the movement of the sense of self into transpersonal realms of consciousness (Singh 1982, p.164). The heightened awareness of both dying and intensive spiritual practice gets "me" out of the way (Singh 1982, p.124).

Fred Grewe, a board-certified chaplain at Providence Hospice in Oregon, created a program called "The Soul's Legacy" (Grewe 2017) as a way to address the most important quality-of-life indicators at the end of life. These indicators include "being able to help others, making a difference in the lives of those they care about, saying important things to loved ones, having a sense of meaning, and sharing with family, including times together, gifts and wisdom" (Grewe 2017, p.3). The "Soul's Legacy" is a five-week interactive group program with weekly assignments focused on "connecting with your soul, connecting with your story, connecting with the Divine, connecting with others, and connecting with mortality" (Grewe 2017, p.10), with the goal of creating a "personal blessing to be given to specific loved ones" (Grewe 2017, p.3). Grewe discovered through a pre- and post-program questionnaire that creating a "Soul's Legacy" alleviated existential distress. He also discovered that sharing one's story in a group setting "promotes fertile soil for a deepening of relationships" whereby most of the participants wanted to continue meeting after the program ended (Grewe 2017, pp.10–11).

Creating an "ethical will" or "*Zava'ah*" in Hebrew, is a way of passing down ethical values between generations. This ancient tradition has evolved over the years to also include personal reflections, values and ideals. These documents are also referred to as "spiritual wills," "personal legacy documents," and "legacy letters." Regardless of what they are called, they all have one important thing in common: "to pass on wisdom and love" (Burket n.d.). Sometimes a person will write his or her own obituary as a way to express their most valued life contributions.

David Isay is the founder of The StoryCorps Project, whose "mission is to preserve and share humanity's stories in order to build connections between people and create a more just and compassionate world." In *Listening is an Act of Love*, he writes:

> *[I]f we take the time to listen, we'll find wisdom, wonder, and poetry in the lives and stories of the people all around us…we all want to know our lives have mattered and we won't ever be forgotten…listening is an act of Love. (Isay 2007, p.1)*

It can be difficult for some to articulate their sense of the Divine or to express love or the need for reconciliation. The ability to express emotions and to sense the metaphysical is often easier through the written word. In her book, *Lasting Words: A Guide to Find Meaning toward the Close of Life*, Claire Willis describes the importance of words at the end of one's life:

> *Perhaps words never matter more than they do at the end of life. For the past 20 years, I have led writing groups for people with life-threatening diseases. I have seen up close the healing power of words, both for the writer and for those receiving their words. People with only days or months to live want to explore*

spiritual issues and engage in a search for deeper meaning of their lives. Using writing for that exploration offered them a particular kind of solitude to sort through their most personal thoughts and feelings… When people are at or near the end of life, they may turn to writing as a way of speaking to loved ones to address unresolved questions and as a means of offering a gift or legacy to those they are leaving behind. The words from these days may be the most valuable gift that can be given to individuals who are dying, a window into themselves that perhaps they were never able to share. (Willis 2013, pp.1–2)

The written word may be in the form of a story, letter, poem, or a journal entry. If a person is unable to write, their words may be dictated or recorded. Some hospices have established oral history programs which allow patients to tell their stories and preserve them, much like the David Isay's StoryCorps Project (Puchalski 2006, p.314). Tonia Colleen Martin, is an author, painter, and poet who "believes writing to be an act of incarnation," which is to "make something live inside something that was formerly dead…a kind of joining between the profane and the sacred… The resulting story relegated to fluttering paper echoes that of the human soul" (Martin 2016, p.62).

Capps argues that "the theology of hope seems much closer to artistic forms of projection than to religious ones… we should not be surprised that poets are able to give us a richer collection of God images than theologians" (Capps 1995, p.67). He adds that "because this projection does not assign a fixed and immutable trait to God, or even a fixed identity to God, it implies that the future itself is open to new possibilities" (Capps 1995, p.68).

Poetry and other forms of writing are powerful ways to cultivate *Hope-in-the-present-moment*. Robert McDowell created a guide for using poetry as a spiritual path. He defines poetry as a "spiritual practice [that] requires unwavering presence in the moment" (McDowell 2008, p.6). According to the poet and professor Mark Burrows, "[p]oems thicken our visual experience of what we sometimes blandly call reality" (Burrows 2016, p.46). The Franciscan priest, Richard Rohr, writes:

> *[P]oetry can help us connect with our True Self, uninhibited by ego's need for certitude or security... Before 500 BCE, religion and poetry were largely the same thing. People did not presume to be able to define the Mystery. They looked for words that could describe the Mystery. Poetry doesn't claim to be perfect as dogma foolishly does. (Rohr n.d.)*

Elegies, which are poems written to praise the dead, are a powerful spiritual tool (McDowell 2008). McDowell further describes an elegy as not only about the dead but also about the writer. "It is an emotional acknowledgement on his or her part that all things are impermanent which is itself a profound spiritual understanding" (McDowell 2008, p.216) and "is all about closing the gap between the visible and invisible world" (McDowell 2008, p.218). The following poem is an elegy written by a young man following the death of his mother.

Poem for Mom

A cheerful memory can brighten one's day
The power to make a sunny day out of skies of gray

Imagining the gleam of your smile
Gave me joy for quite a while

And the white of your teeth
Subdued sorrow that is now pushed deep beneath
Don't let me forget, the perk of your grin
To describe how you make me feel within
I wouldn't know where to begin
Altogether your countenance
Inspired in ways I can't count
And hence—
The pretense
Of this day
Shall be that of celebrating sunlight,
Opposed to drab gray

There are no sunny days, without ominous storms
There is no light without darkness
No growth without decay
No life without death

As pollution allows us to see the magnificent colors of
a sunset
So death allows us to appreciate the beauty of your life

I see you in the colors of the sky
I hear you in the songs of the birds
I feel you looking over me
You are the sunshine on my shoulders

You are no longer with us
Yet you're now with us more than ever
Your life ceases
But your life only multiplies

It's a funny thing
How the value of art increases posthumous
This is because it is seen as a piece of the artist

And the greatness of an artist is only felt in full when the
artist is no longer with us

I now feel my life has much more importance
As I know you live on in me
I hope to keep making you proud
Until the day I'll be with you again, like I know I'll be

Noah Holman, 2018

Music, dance, and the visual arts

In her book *A Time for Listening and Caring: Spirituality and the Care of the Chronically Ill and Dying*, Puchalski emphasizes the importance of music, dance, and the visual arts as healing modalities at the end-of-life. Puchalski writes: "As each of us face the waterfalls ahead, may our hearts sing and our wings unfold to the music, the music that reminds us of what matters most" (Puchalski 2006, p.330). She illustrates her own personal journey in understanding the power of art in healing. At the age of 37, she found herself on the edge of the abyss after being diagnosed with breast cancer while still breastfeeding her third child:

[A]s I struggled to find some comfort in sleep, I found myself having a "waking dream." There in the darkness of my room, with my young family asleep, an odd notion kept pressing me to rise and dance... I had actually stopped dancing to pursue medicine—it seemed strange that a part of me, so long forgotten, reared up as a pathway to explore my illness. That night, I went to the other end of the house and put on some music and danced in tears... I recall feeling an opening through which my essential Self rose along with the rhythms of

the music—feeling in unison with something far greater than myself—not alone. (Puchalski 2006, p.303)

Puchalski describes how dance helped her discover *Hope-in* the midst of suffering. The arts experience "is one that moves us or elevates us to a higher sense of ourselves and others. This elevation seems to connect us with something or someone beyond our normal realm" (Puchalski 2006, p.303). This is why dance has always played an important role in religious practices, including but not limited to liturgical dance in Christian churches, the Native American pow wow, and the whirling dervishes of the Sufi Islamic sects. A liturgical dancer, Carla de Sola, defines dance as a way to explore mystery, saying, "the dancer who moves with an open and generous heart communicates a sense of warmth and inclusiveness that envelops all within it" (De Sola 2001, p.154). A dancer is able to discover "something on a nonverbal level about their relationship with the world, the self, and God…this leads to a new level of spiritual enrichment" (De Sola 2001, p.163).

When we think of dance we think of movement whereby a body is engaged in its fullest physical capacity. Puchalski stresses that this does not limit dance in patients who have significant limitations:

Even though the limbs of the body may be limited, dance therapy offers the person a means for soul expression, and any movement, even as simple as lifting a hand, can be infinitely significant. Even when one is unable to move the limbs, there is also a response in the body, for there is movement inside the body: muscles of the throat contract, the eyes flutter while the blood dances in the body. These silent movements can occur when both therapist and client are in the state of "what is," a reality in the end if life reflecting the immediacy of life... In this sense music and dance are ideal communicators of Truth, since the body doesn't lie...movement reveals the soul, and what better therapy to employ...than a model that seeks to embrace a client exactly as he or she is, in the Now, without artifice. (Puchalski 2006, p.286)

The key message in Puchalski's writing is clear: We need to accept our bodies just the way they are in a given moment in time. This is what the theologian Elisabeth Moltmann-Wendel, coveys in her book *I Am My Body*. She explores the theology of embodiment through a feminist lens. She describes that the theology of embodiment:

[s]eeks to give people once again the courage to use their senses, which atrophy in a rational culture, to stand by themselves and their experiences and accept themselves with their bodies, to love them, to trust them and their understanding, and to see themselves as children of this earth, indissolubly bound up with it...the beginning and end of all God's works is embodiment. (Moltmann-Wendel 1995, pp.104–5)

Moltmann-Wendel emphasizes the importance of touch:

From the first to the last day, touching is experienced as assurance, confirmation of the self and healing...to touch means to stimulate people in their whole existence, with their senses and their spirits, heal their brokenness and make them once again capable of contact, thought and experience. (Moltmann-Wendel 1995, pp.64–5)

Dance can be as simple as holding another person's hand while listening to music.

Puchalski further discusses how meaning in one's life can also be discovered through music (Puchalski 2006). "Music reaches to the center of our being and gives form and meaning to life, but it also gives a partial revelation: a glimpse of God" (Black 2004, p.195). Music has a special affinity for taking us into a different realm, helping to cultivate a sense of *Hope-in* knowing there is something greater than ourselves. Music can also play a role in fostering *Hope-in-the-present-moment.*

For anyone, music that touches the heart is deeply calming, making it more possible for those surrounded by such music to embrace an attitude of compassion, acceptance, and presence. (Puchalski 2006, p.320)

Capps describes music as having:

A unique association with hoping...it is no accident that images of hope are found preeminently in the psalms, which are, after all, songs of hymns. Nor is it surprising that the transition from our present life to the life that awaits us after death is most effectively portrayed through music. (Capps 1995, p.45)

Music therapy and music thanatology are used to help alleviate suffering and help a person as they transition from life to death:

Music connects us to the unseen part of us, the part of us that crosses between worlds...music is a magnet into the mystery, a guide to the unknown. Thus music reminds us of this

ephemeral soul of ours, summoning unseen wings with which
we can soar. (Puchalski 2006, p.322)

It is important to encourage patients and their loved ones to
let go, use their imaginations and let the Spirit move them.
This allows the process of producing or experiencing art as
a way of cultivating *Hope-in-the-present-moment*. Deborah
Sokolove, Director of the Henry Luce III Center for the Arts
and Religion at Wesley Theological Seminary, and Professor
of Art and Worship, describes *Hope-in-the-present-moment*
through art in this way:

> *[T]he primary use of art is simply to be itself. Just as we are*
> *commanded to keep the Sabbath, not in order to be more*
> *productive, but to rest our bodies and our souls, to simply*
> *delight in the presence of God, so are we given the capacity and*
> *the yearning for art. In our results-driven world, we have to*
> *tell ourselves to consciously slow down, to pay attention,*
> *to listen for God's voice. Like sitting on the front porch of a*
> *retreat lodge and staring at the tree line, or strolling along the*
> *seashore watching the waves go in and out, participation in*
> *the arts—whether as a practitioner or as audience—has the*
> *potential to open us to a wider, deeper reality. (Sokolove 2013,*
> *pp.161–2)*

Sokolove emphasizes art as a powerful medium that gives us
the ability to experience God. Art helps us to cultivate our
sense of *Hope-in* a power greater than ourselves:

> *But like worship, the arts need have no purpose except to bring*
> *us closer to God, to operate as a channel by which God's love*
> *is made real to us. They do this by stopping us in our tracks,*

inviting us to be still, to attend, to pay attention to what is immediately before us. As invitations to live into the present moment in all its fullness, the arts can heal broken hearts, feed starving souls, and clothe the ineffable in garments of matter.
(Sokolove 2013, pp.168–9)

Curtis Thompson, Professor at The University of Chicago School of Divinity, stresses the importance of imagination in the arts in order for translucence to take place. He defines translucence as "a 'shining through'," from the Latin verb *translucere*; it suggests the "capability of the natural and human worlds to allow God's light to shine through… God is both the origin and the content of the world's translucence: the world is translucent to God's very reality" (Thompson 2004, p.3). He adds that "the reality of the imagination delivers us to the realm of possibility, which in turn is the gateway to the eternal" (Thompson 2004, p.37).

According to Wilson Yates, the twentieth-century German theologian Paul Tillich also understood art as vital means of spiritual expression. Yates speaks of Tillich's belief that art was "a means through which the religious story could be told and spiritual meaning could be experienced… More than science or philosophy, art provided the window into the human condition that theology needed to look through" (Yates 2015, p.37).

Expressing oneself through art can be a practice of meditation or *Hope-in-the-present-moment*. Frederick Frank (1973), beautifully captures this concept in his book *The Zen of Seeing: Seeing/Drawing as Meditation*. Frank illustrates a technique he calls seeing/drawing, whereby the purpose is not to produce a replica of what is seen. Instead, it is letting "seeing/drawing be the celebration of experiencing, of the eye in love, instead of making of pictures to be framed" (Frank

1973, p.24). The purpose is to draw based on really seeing what is in front of you and drawing without looking at what you are drawing. He describes seeing/drawing as a "technique of contemplation. The eye, heart, hand become one with what is seen and drawn, things are seen as they are—in their 'isness.' Seeing things thus, I know who I am!" (Frank 1973, p.15).

Other artists describe how art brings one into the present moment. Daniel Siedell, in his book *God in the Gallery: A Christian Embrace of Modern Art*, recounts how James Lee Byars, a contemporary artist who began his career in the 1950s, had a goal "to make himself disappear or dissolve into his work in order to focus on the experience of the present, which his artworks and performances were to celebrate" (Siedell 2008, p.97).

Thomas Merton, a twentieth-century Trappist monk, stressed art as an important element of contemplative prayer and meditation:

> *The function of image, symbol, poetry, music, chant, and of ritual (remotely related to sacred dance) is to open up the inner self of the contemplative, to incorporate the senses and the body in the totality of the self-orientation to God that is necessary for worship and meditation. Simply to neglect the senses and body altogether, and merely to let the imagination go its own way, while attempting to plunge into a deeply abstracted interior prayer, will end in no result even for one who is proficient in meditation. (Merton 1990, p.85)*

Meditation, centering prayer and rituals

Meditation helps us to let go of our egos and experience God or the Divine in the present moment. Singh describes that meditation is mindfulness (Singh 1982). Meditation works by helping us to let go of our "personal self" (Singh 1982, p.118). She stresses that the personal self or ego is stubborn and wants to be in control. It is important to take time for meditation and contemplation in order to move beyond the ego—to simply just be (p.66). She further states:

> *The continued practice of present-centered awareness, in time, simply wears away the ego...our ego has always attempted to find meaning in life through doing...moving beyond the ego is moving beyond meaning defined by doing and move into meaning by being. This is a painful point for many with terminal illness who have always found their value in doing... To realize that all we have is the present moment, that all we can do is be, is an insight of considerable depth for ordinary people, just like us, who live most of our lives at a great distance from the Real. (Singh 1982, pp.126–8)*

Deborah Norris, Director of the Psychobiology of Healing Program at American University and founder of the Mindfulness Center, also describes meditation as being mindful of the present moment and being part of the Real which she refers to as *the flow*:

> *What we notice when we explore our experience of being in the moment is actually more like a sense of flow; a sense of ever-shifting rhythms around us...when not in the flow we find our thoughts directed towards the future. Concerns about the future can lead to apprehension, anxiety, and stress...another possibility is that our thoughts are directed towards the past. In this case, we may spend time in remorse or regret...in the flow, we do not experience these judgmental feelings of the past or*

the future. Curiosity about the experience of the ever-moving flow evolves to senses of awe and wonder. Our consciousness fill with a sense of peace as we synchronize with the momentum of the flow in and around us. (Norris 2017, p.7)

She suggests that a chosen space to practice meditation is a sanctuary (Norris 2017). Puchalski also explains that a sense of a sanctuary occurs because the contemplation that takes place in meditation creates a space where one encounters the Divine:

[This] gives one deeper knowledge and understanding of who God or the Divine is...prayer and meditation are the experiences of being in relationship with God or the Divine. At times, during prayer and meditation, one can experience union and oneness with God and the Divine. (Puchalski 2006, p.60)

Borg defines this experience of deep meditation as having "a sense of entering the presence of God or even becoming absorbed into God" (Borg 1997, p.40). For the twentieth-century Jewish philosopher Martin-Buber, this sense of being in the presence of God is described as the *I–Thou* relationship. Buber further asserts these experiences as a type of *Hope-with* because the sense of being in relationship with God can occur during any encounter with God's creations, human or otherwise (Borowitz 1983).

Thomas Merton wrote that "contemplative souls generally have a special attraction to the presence of God within them, or to some other form of consciousness of God's nearness to their intimate being" (Merton 1960, p.76). Singh describes this as "the experience of the body as the 'temple of God,'" and reminds us that the "true meaning of the word contemplation

[is] completely, to make a temple, completely, to make a holy space" (Singh 1982, p.139).

Influenced by Merton and other great contemplators, Thomas Keating, a Cistercian priest, monk, and abbot, became the founder of the Centering Prayer Movement and of Contemplative Outreach. Keating defines centering prayer as a type of contemplative prayer, both of which are types of meditation practices (Keating 2002). He writes that centering prayer is a practice that helps us to develop our relationship with God and brings us to the level of "pure faith" (Keating 2002, p.13). The more we let go, "the stronger the presence of the Spirit becomes. The Ultimate Mystery becomes the Ultimate presence" (Keating 2002, p.17). He stresses that:

> *The chief thing that separates us from God is the thought that we are separated from Him…we fail to believe that we are always with God and that He is part of every reality. The present moment, every object we see, our in-most nature are all rooted in Him…contemplative prayer is a way of awakening to the reality to which we are immersed.… Interior silence is the perfect seed bed for divine love to take root. (Keating 2002, pp.44–5)*

The Buddhist monk, Thich Nhat Hanh, in his book *Living Buddha, Living Christ*, emphasizes the fact that being in the present moment is the best way to cultivate hope:

> *In Buddhism, we speak of touching nirvana with our own body. In Christianity, you can also touch the Kingdom of God with your body, right here and now. It is much safer than placing our hope in the future. If we cling to our idea of hope in the future, we might not notice the peace and joy that are*

available in the present moment. The best way to take care of the future is to take care of the present moment. Practicing conscious breathing, aware of each thought and each act, we are reborn, fully alive, in the present moment…unless we channel our energies toward being aware of what is going on in the present moment, we might not discover the peace and happiness available to us right now. The well within us. If we dig deeply into the present moment, the water will spring forth. (Hanh 2007, p.179)

Jon Kabat-Zinn, a physician, author, and meditation teacher, sums it up this way: "[W]hen we let go of wanting something else to happen in this moment, we are taking a profound step toward being able to encounter the here now" (Kabat-Zinn 1994, p.15). Later, in the same book, he writes, "So, in meditation practice, the best way to get somewhere is to let go of trying to get anywhere at all" (Kabat-Zinn 1994, p.16). This is what it is to be mindful. To be aware of this very moment and no other moment. To be exactly where you are now.

Jacobson speaks of the importance of cultivating *Hope-in-the-present-moment* through mindfulness to help ease the fear of death:

The only way you can know death is with your mind. You can anticipate death, which creates a fear of death, but death never arrives. It only approaches. If you relax and remain present, and you do not anticipate what is approaching, then there is only this moment and, in this moment, there is no death. There is only life. (Jacobson 2007, p.220)

Keating also describes the use of meditation and centering prayer to ease the fear of death:

*In deep prayer you do not think about the body anyway.
The prospect of dying is not threatening because you have
experienced a preview of what it might be like for your spirit
to be separated from your body, and it is delightful. (Keating
2002, p.61)*

This concept of lessening the fear of dying through meditation
is the major theme woven into Singh's book *The Grace in Dying*.
According to Singh, meditation "seeks to imitate the stages of
dying so that we may learn to die while we are still alive" (Singh
1982, p.166). The same is true for someone who is dying. She
describes that with both meditation and dying we deeply and
completely enter the present moment and beyond to a place
where there is no concept of time or space (Singh 1982, p.82).
She adds that grace is "the experience of finally, gratefully,
relaxing the contraction of fearful separation and opening to
the Spirit as our own radiant splendor: Knowing it, feeling it,
entering it as it enters us (Singh 1982, pp.82). She writes, "We
move beyond our human sense of history, our past and our
fleeting present and our future, into pure Being, moments of
Presence that are eternal, beyond time, that are everlastingly,
exhilaratingly *now* (Singh 1982, p.111).

Rituals are another way to cultivate hope at the end-of-
life—not only *Hope-in* and *Hope-in-the-present-moment*, but
also *Hope-with*. They can help guide people in their transition
from *Hope-that* a cure will be found to *Hope-that* they will
experience a peaceful death. Puchalski states, "Every culture
has developed rituals to guide its members through significant
transitions in their lives, including dying" (Puchalski 2006,
p.245). According to Anderson:

> *Rituals help heal the pain of letting go, offering reconciliation and peace, while at the same time connecting us with the divine. It has been my experience that end-of-life rituals can help a person die not only a peaceful death, but also a sacred death, bringing reconciliation and acceptance to both the loved ones and the person dying. (Anderson 2003, p.19)*

In his book *Liberation Rites: Understanding the Transformative Power of Ritual,* Tom Driver writes:

> *When people engage in ritual activity, they separate themselves, partially if not totally, from the roles and status they have in the workday world. There is a threshold in time or space or both, and certainly a demarcation of behavior, over which people pass when entering into a ritual. (Driver 2006, p.159)*

Driver describes ritual as cultivating *Hope-in,* whereby the participants transcend beyond the present time and space. He refers to this as "liminality" (Driver 2006, pp.158–9). Ritual also cultivates *Hope-with,* because it "not only brings people together in a physical assembly but also tends to unite them emotionally" (Driver 2006, p.152). According to Puchalski, "rituals acknowledge the presence of the Holy, bless relationships, and foster a sense of security and continuity in the face of an unknown future" (Puchalski 2006. pp.153–4). Rituals also help to cultivate *Hope-in-the-present-moment*: "Rituals are meant to be ageless and timeless, bringing the needs of participants into the present situation" (Anderson 2003, p.20).

For some, traditional rituals performed by their religious leader may be essential, especially for members of an orthodox faith. For example, most practicing Catholics desire to receive the Sacrament of the Anointing of the Sick from their priest. Puchalski notes, "For Catholics the sacraments are a sign of God's presence" (Puchalski 2006, p.150). However, Anderson stresses that it is important to recognize that traditional rituals prescribed by a faith tradition may not always meet a person's needs. She observes that "all too often, traditional religious rituals fail to provide satisfying closure, either because clergy are not always available to assist in these rites or the rites themselves have lost significance for the participants" (Anderson 2003, p.20). Therefore, creating a new ritual for a patient and their loved ones is a vital role for a chaplain to consider when discovering ways to cultivate hope at the end-of-life.

Susan Smith, an Episcopal priest, stresses the importance of developing authentic, life-giving rituals in her book *Caring Liturgies: The Pastoral Power of Christian Ritual.* She describes that a ritual done well can "create unity out of estrangement, support out of isolation, and hope out of fear or despair" (Smith 2012, p.3). On the other hand, a ritual done poorly by calling attention to itself causes both the flow and the power to be broken (Smith 2012). Just as with meditation, it's important to get the ego out of the way because "[t]o enable God's power requires avoiding ego power" (Smith 2012, p.8). She also emphasizes the importance of prayer, being open to the Spirit, and deep listening when developing a ritual (Smith 2012). It is also important for the dying person to be the focal point. This is stressed by both Smith (2012) and Anderson:

Sacred dying rituals are primarily and notably for the person dying. It takes great strength and courage to face death and to begin to move through it to the other side. And it takes great courage for the survivors to put aside their own fears

and anxieties to help their loved ones die a peaceful death.
(Anderson 2003, p.44)

Even though the focal point is the dying person, Smith also describes the *Hope-with* that is cultivated through a ritual done well, calling ritual a group experience. She notes that "like good conversation, at the end people feel refreshed and satisfied, for they have participated in something greater than themselves, something uplifting, something true and honest" (Smith 2012, p.102). She further adds that to be "true and honest" a ritual must "allow the depth of lament and the height of joy abide together, in preparation and then in the ritual so that (like a concerto) honest hope may be celebrated in the end" (Smith 2012, p.104). For Smith, ritual works below the level of conscious awareness, noting that "ritual does not explain but enacts the real... When spiritually, fluently, and competently done, ritual can care for someone's mind, body, and soul" (Smith 2012, p.138).

The role of the chaplain

One of the gifts that a chaplain often brings to the dying is their undivided attention and willingness to listen to a person's life story. A life review allows one to cultivate *Hope-in* as they discover the contributions they have made and the legacy they will leave behind.

The chaplain may encourage a person to capture their emotions and life stories in writing as a narrative, letter, or poem. For those who are unable to write, another way to capture and preserve their story is through an audio recording. StoryCorps now has an "app" that allows people to submit and archive their story remotely.

Encouraging patients and their loved ones to express themselves and to experience *Hope-in-the-present-moment* through the visual arts can be as simple as providing colored pencils and paper. More complex expressions may involve painting, scrapbooking, knitting, or the making of prayer beads. Producing tangible items that a patient is able to give away also helps to cultivate *Hope-in* by contributing to their sense of legacy.

Some patients may wish to express themselves through music. Music can be either experienced or played depending on the individual. For many, familiar music can provide a source of relaxation and comfort and can be a portal to *Hope-in*.

Friends, family, and even hospital staff may also benefit from experiencing the arts along with the patient to help them process their feelings. This is another way to foster *Hope-with*. Finally, by being able to express one's innermost feelings through art, the shift from *Hope-that* a cure will be found can gradually shift to *Hope-that* their death will be peaceful.

Cultivating *Hope-that, Hope-in, Hope-with* and *Hope-in-the-present-moment* through meditation, contemplative prayer, and ritual, benefits everyone involved because preparing for death should be a part of life. To make this point, Anderson quotes the Scottish novelist Muriel Spark:

> *If I had to live my life over again, I would for the habit of nightly composing my thoughts of death. I would practice, as it were, the remembrance of death. There is no other practice which so intensifies life. Death, when it approaches, ought not to take one by surprise. It should be part of the full expectancy of life. (Muriel Spark, quoted in Anderson 2003, p.18)*

Centering prayer is a practice that can be easily taught to patients. Keating describes the process of centering prayer in a few simple steps: Get into a comfortable position, close your eyes, think of a sacred word that is a "symbol of your intention to open yourself into the mystery of God's presence beyond thoughts, images and emotions" (Keating 2002, p.110). Return to your sacred word whenever ordinary thoughts enter your mind and let the ordinary thoughts drift away like boats on the water.

There are also simple meditation methods that can be taught to patients who do not have a particular faith tradition or who may be non-religious. The most basic meditation is the practice of focusing on the breath. As Singh says, "As we become more mindful of our breathing, we become increasingly present" (Singh 1982, p.149). There are numerous scripts available to help guide patients through a meditation. At times a script may not be necessary and, by using one's imagination, the chaplain can incorporate language and metaphors common to a patient's religious background, as appropriate. The key is to be open, trust, and be guided by the Spirit. This is also true when creating a ritual. As Smith and Anderson point out, it is important to keep the focus on the one who is dying and, and the same time, invite others into full participation. When done well, the result of a ritual should be that of an *I–Thou* experience.

Summary

There are a variety of ways a chaplain can help cultivate hope at the end-of-life. This chapter offers a brief overview of some of the many possibilities. By actively listening, a chaplain can explore what brings meaning to people's lives and, in turn, help to transform meaning into dimensions of hope through storytelling, art, music, meditation, and ritual. Through active listening and creative partnership with the Spirit, the opportunities are limitless.

CHAPTER 4

Hope, Spiritual Assessment, and Plan of Care

A number of spiritual assessment tools have been developed for gathering spiritual information (Saguil and Phelps 2012). Often mnemonics are used to help clinicians remember specific questions to ask. One example is the HOPE questionnaire. The categories covered in this tool are listed as follows: H stands for "[s]ources of hope, meaning, comfort, strength, peace, love, connection"; O stands for "organized religion"; P stands for "personal spirituality and practices"; and E stands for "[e]ffects on medical care and end-of-life decisions" (Anandarajah and Height 2002, p.86). Once obtained from the patient, the information can easily be organized into one or more of the four dimensions of hope. This provides a framework for the data to be analyzed and allows a plan of care to be developed for each patient.

The following examples demonstrate how to organize patient information into dimensions of hope and write a plan of care based on this analysis. A formal questionnaire was not used; however, if one were to use a questionnaire, the process would be the same. The following examples are based on actual encounters I experienced as a chaplain intern and hospice chaplain. Some details have been altered out of respect for patient privacy. Note that the dimensions of hope are included in *italic* in the assessment and the plan of care to demonstrate the use of hope as a framework. They are not meant to be written in the actual documentation.

Ms. L, a 62-year-old Asian female with metastatic ovarian cancer

When I met Ms. L she had been admitted to in-patient hospice for pain management. Although she welcomed a chaplain visit, Ms. L was quick to inform me that she was not religious. After a brief conversation about her admission and illness, she opened up and spoke of her beliefs about God and the afterlife. She shared with me that she did have faith in God and the belief that something will happen in the next life. Even though she didn't know what the next life entailed, she trusted that she would be "okay." During our visit, Ms. L spoke about being at peace since she had prepared for her death and had all her affairs in order. She described having close relationships with several friends and her two adult daughters. She knew her daughters would miss her but believed that they would adjust since they were both very independent. She said she didn't care about the details of a memorial service but she did want her ashes spread on the east and west coasts. Then she shifted the conversation saying, "I really don't want to talk about death anymore. I know it's going to happen. I did all my crying and now I just want to live each day the best I can." As our visit came to a close, she eagerly showed me her wooden Happy Buddha statue. The statue could stand upright or upside down. She explained that she changed his position depending on how she was feeling. When she was happy, she put him upside down. I asked her how she would like him today, and she said, "Let's put him upside down." She was receptive to hearing a prayer and appeared peaceful at the close of our visit.

Ms. L was an encounter most chaplains love to have. She was open, honest, and engaging. Although she was not religious, she was very spiritual, and her future story about the afterlife was comforting to her even though she did not have a definitive concept. Her *Hope-that* a cure would be found clearly shifted to *Hope-that* she would have a peaceful death. She also had *Hope-that* her daughters would be fine knowing she had her affairs in orders and had raised them to be self-sufficient. She had *Hope-in* as evidenced by her belief in God and an afterlife, and spoke of *Hope-with* in relation to her friendship, daughters, and her simple ritual of positioning the Happy Buddha statue according to her mood. Finally, it was evident that Ms. L found *Hope-in-the-present-moment* as she described her shift from her thinking about death to thinking about living each day the best way she could.

* * *

Based on this assessment, there does not appear to be any dimensions of hope that have not been cultivated. Therefore, the plan of care for Ms. L may include the following:

- Continue allowing her to spend as much time as possible with her friends and family (*Hope-with*).

- Continue to give her the opportunity to live each day in whatever way she chooses (*Hope-in-the-present-moment*).

- Continue to ensure her pain is well managed so she can trust that she will have a peaceful death (*Hope-that*).

- Reinforce her spiritual beliefs by offering prayer that includes her belief in God, the mystery of an afterlife and the legacy she will pass onto her daughters (*Hope-in*).

Ms. D, a 68-year-old black female with metastatic liver cancer

I met Ms. D when I was a chaplain intern at a large medical center in Baltimore, Maryland. She was admitted with abdominal pain and weight loss, and during her hospitalization she was diagnosed with metastatic liver cancer. I was asked to see her because she was extremely anxious. Her demographics listed her as Catholic. She tearfully welcomed me into her room and immediately began to express her fear of dying. I have to admit, as a new chaplain, I was not very confident in my ability to help her. I knew the best thing I could offer her was to simply listen to her concerns; however, Ms. D had another agenda. She asked me many difficult questions about the Christian tradition. Then she shared with me her vision of seeing Jesus at a time in her life when she was desperately in need of help. She claimed that Jesus had appeared to her and questioned why he didn't come to her now when she needed him the most. I visited Ms. D frequently, and each time she repeated the same questions: "If Jesus is really God, why did he cry out for God to help him when he was on the cross? Why did Jesus pray to God, if Jesus is really God? Why would Jesus pray to himself?" I was honest and explained that my inability to provide her answers was due to my inexperience and limited knowledge, since I was only in my second year of seminary. I honestly believed I would have the answers to these questions after completing Systematic Theology the following semester. Of course, that was not the case, as I soon discovered many well-constructed opinions but no absolute answers. I encouraged Ms. D to ask the priest these same questions when he came to offer her Holy Communion. To my disappointment she never did.

Most of my visits with Ms. D involved her rapid-fire questions. She became accustomed to my not having the answers and would seldom pause for a response. I was often able to divert the conversation to her family to assess her support systems. She was very close to her son and concerned about how he was handling her illness. She confided in me that her daughter-in-law was a recovering heroin addict who was now very frail. She expressed her concern that her son spent much of his time and energy caring for her. Each time I visited Ms. D, she would ask me why Jesus "still hadn't shown up." As new treatment options were presented to her, she began to ask my opinion on whether or not she should receive treatment, considering the severity of her cancer. I would try to deflect these questions back to her by inquiring what she believed to be the best option.

On the last day we met, her son and daughter-in-law were visiting her. It was my first time meeting them. Ms. D's son was obviously very close to her and reassured her not to worry as he would take good care of her. As he spoke to his mother, I realized that Ms. D was not aware that Jesus actually did "show up." Jesus was right there in front of her, reflected in the love she was receiving from her own son. I emphasized this point in my final prayer with her.

As we said our goodbyes, I told Ms. D that I hoped she enjoyed school because she was coming with me. She seemed a bit confused until I explained that I planned to ask all her questions to my Systematic Theology professor. Ms. D smiled and tearfully hugged me goodbye.

Ms. D is a perfect example of someone who was reconstructing her theology in response to a crisis. She was raised Catholic and much of what she was taught in her childhood no longer made sense to her. She was working hard to cultivate her *Hope-in*. She had a strong sense of Jesus but struggled to find peace in trusting that which she could not see. As various treatment options were being presented to her, she spoke of *Hope-that* in terms of receiving chemotherapy, even though the palliative care team was very candid about the improbability of a cure. Their candidness and assurance of pain control helped her to think about the *Hope-that* she would have a peaceful death. She found a tremendous amount of *Hope-with* in her relationship with her son. I was not made aware of her other support systems. I did know that she was a non-practicing Catholic and was not a member of a congregation. She never mentioned her desire to become reconnected with her faith tradition in a formal sense. Her candid theological reflection indicated that she was a woman with a strong faith in God. Her anxiety about her future story was palpable and there was no evidence that she had cultivated the ability to find *Hope-in-the-present-moment.*

* * *

Based on this assessment, Ms. D's plan of care may include the following:

- Continue to support her as she reconstructs her theology by providing a continuation of chaplaincy care in the outpatient setting (*Hope-in*).

- Encourage her to get her affairs in order (*Hope-that*) and to discover meaning in her life through a life review (*Hope-in*).

- Affirm her close relationship with her son and encourage her to find other resources of support (*Hope-with*).

- Honor her treatment decisions and help to ensure her symptoms are well managed (*Hope-that*).

- Discover ways to help decrease her anxiety through guided meditation, praying the rosary, listening to music, writing poetry, or in other ways that will help her to express herself and embrace the moment she is in (*Hope-in-the-present-moment*).

Mr. S, a 58-year-old white male with end stage liver disease

Mr. S was admitted to the inpatient hospice, at his own request, in order to be separated from his family during the holidays. He felt estranged from his family even though he was living in his sister's home. He welcomed me into his room and offered me a seat. After introducing myself as one of the hospice chaplains, Mr. S stated that he no longer believed in God and "when you die, that's it…you're gone." Then he added that "once you're gone, eventually everyone forgets you, no matter how important or famous you are." He began to talk about his family and his inability to understand them. He described his living situation as unbearable and wished he had never moved in with his sister. He spoke about his life in New York City and his love of traveling, which he could no longer do. He dreaded having to return to his sister's home after the holidays and was unable to find anything about the situation that provided him comfort. He reported that he did not have a support system in the immediate area, and any suggestions to help him improve his situation were quickly negated. I spent most of the time listening to his complaints. To my surprise, he allowed me to offer a prayer. I started the prayer addressing the Spirit of Life and reflected on much of what I had heard, emphasizing my hope in his ability to find his living situation more tolerable. I focused on his ability to find *Hope-in*: a hope within himself not dependent on others. I prayed that he would be able to discover an inner peace that would be with him regardless of his situation. When I finished the prayer, we both sat quietly. He broke the silence by remarking, "You gave me a lot to think about."

Mr. S was an individual who only spoke of the type of hope that depended on the behavior and actions of other people. His only hope was the *Hope-that* his family would change and that would fix his situation. During the hour visit, I heard very little *Hope-with*. He had no friends in the area and spoke briefly about a few friends who still lived in New York. He never described *Hope-in*. He had no future story about death, and he had no belief in a Higher Power, afterlife or a sense that his life had meaning. He described his past career as an artist in New York but believed that nothing he created would be remembered. And finally, there was no evidence that he had done any work to cultivate *Hope-in-the-present-moment*. He no longer painted and never mentioned spending time doing other activities that would help him be in the moment.

* * *

It appeared that Mr. S was not aware of any other dimensions of hope except the *Hope-that* someone else would solve his problems. Therefore, his plan of care may include the following:

- Affirm that he is capable of finding a path to inner peace and help him discover what that would look like for him (*Hope-in*).

- Assist him to find a refuge away from his difficult living situation through meditation, journaling, art, or other creative activities (*Hope-in-the-present-moment*).

- Encourage him to stay connected with his friends in New York and seek other sources of support (*Hope-with*).

Mr. P, a 48-year old Jamaican male with a rare clotting disorder

I met Mr. P in the intensive care unit (ICU) at a university hospital in Washington DC. I was a chaplain intern and on call the night Mr. P's condition worsened. I received the call around 2 am. On my way to seeing the patient, the nurse quickly updated me on his status. He was intubated and was now unresponsive. As a result of poor circulation, he had suffered severe organ failure including damage to his liver and kidneys. Unfortunately, Mr. P had also developed gangrenous extremities. His physician attempted to obtain a Do Not Resuscitate (DNR) order from his family but was unsuccessful. The family had requested to see a chaplain. When I arrived, Mr. P's family and two friends were at the bedside. His wife and two young children were sobbing and pleading "Please don't go." His friends were praying loudly for God to perform a miracle. After introducing myself, they asked me to please pray with them for a miracle. We all held hands as I prayed for healing, comfort, and peace. One of the friends added to the moment by reciting the 23rd psalm followed by the Lord's Prayer. At the close of the visit, the family's pastor arrived. I said my goodbyes knowing they were in good hands.

Chaplains often face calls in the middle of the night asking for miracles. These calls can be difficult. There is little time to get to know the patient or the family and you may never see them again. The ability to do a complete spiritual assessment in these situations is often unrealistic. The only clear assessment in this case was the family's *Hope-that* God would cure their loved one. Asking for a miracle from God is the *Hope-that* something external will fix the problem. There is certainly nothing wrong with asking God for a miracle; however, if that is the only hope that has been cultivated, there is a high potential for a spiritual crisis to occur if the patient dies. Although they believed in God, it was not clear if their relationship with God was also based on *Hope-in*. Mr. P's family and friends desperately wanted God to fix the problem by answering their prayers. But did they also have an internal sense of the Divine with faith and trust in God regardless of the outcome? They had *Hope-with*, as evidenced by their friends and pastor who supported them that night. And finally, having *Hope-in-the-present-moment* is the dimension of hope that is difficult to have in times of crisis. However, it is the hope that can be experienced when one is fully engaged in prayer, and it was clear that prayer was important to this family.

* * *

Based on this assessment, the plan of care may include the following:

- Continue to support the family's need to believe in a miracle and in their treatment decisions (*Hope-that*).

- When appropriate, assist in the transition to hope for a peaceful death (*Hope-that*).

- Incorporate into prayer the trust that God will provide support and strength regardless of the outcome (*Hope-in*).

- Obtain a brief life review and reinforce the patient's legacy as a husband and father (*Hope-in*).

- Reinforce the importance of the support they are receiving from friends, family, and their faith community (*Hope-with*).

- Guide the family to appreciate each moment they spend with Mr. P by talking to him, telling his life stories, and providing him comfort with their gentle touch (*Hope-in-the-present-moment*).

Summary

Writing this book has been an amazing journey of discovery. When I first began this exploration, I understood that there were two dimensions of hope: *Hope-that* and *Hope-in*. Now I have come to realize that there are actually four dimensions of hope: *Hope-that*, *Hope-in*, *Hope-with*, and *Hope-in-the-present moment*.

During my prior career as a nurse practitioner, I came from the medical model that views hope in terms of *Hope-that* a cure will be found. As a new chaplain intern, I found myself overwhelmed by the concept of hope. I now understand the importance of *Hope-in* and the chaplain's role in helping guide people as they reconstruct their embedded theology into a deliberative theology of hope. I have also come to recognize the importance of *Hope-with* as I witness the Divine power of love. And, finally though self-discovery, I have come to recognize the importance of *Hope-in-the-present-moment*.

One could argue that *Hope-in-the-present-moment* is a type of *Hope-in*; however, I believe *Hope-in-the-present-moment* is the foundation of all hope and probably the most important one to cultivate. I believe it is what Rumbold describes as a "mature hope." Rumbold stresses that "mature hope" takes time and is something we should nurture throughout our life (Rumbold 1986, pp.66–7). Stephen Levine, Leonard Jacobson, Kathleen Singh, and other teachers of meditation stress that the ability to be in the present moment is essential for living well and dying well. Jacobson says: "Death is not something to be afraid of. What is to be feared is to not live life fully" (Jacobson 2007, p.223). Puchalski also emphasizes the importance of preparing for our death throughout our lives (Puchalski 2006).

When I reflect on the time I spent with Abby, my friend and former colleague, I believe it was Divine intervention that our paths crossed again at a pivotal time. I was a new and inexperienced chaplain intern. Abby was a young social scientist who studied hope in cancer patients in her post-doctorate work prior to replacing me when I retired from the FDA. In her research, she discovered that stories about "underdogs" achieving success gave cancer patients the greatest sense of hope (Prestin 2013). When she, herself, was diagnosed with a cancer that reoccurred despite aggressive treatment, she expressed to me her frustration in her lack of ability to remain hopeful. Abby had read about a woman who had undergone 14 different types of cancer treatments until one was finally successful. She struggled to understand how this woman was able to remain hopeful for so long. Abby was desperately hanging onto the *Hope-that* another treatment would be found for her. At that time, I also found myself capable of only thinking in terms of *Hope-that* another treatment would be available. *Hope-in, Hope-with,* or *Hope-in-the-present-moment* did not even occur to me. I, too, felt hopeless.

During this exploration on hope, I would often replay in my head how I would have done things differently. Most likely, Abby would have continued her quest to find the next treatment. Since this is what gave her hope, I would never take that away from her. However, when she would ask me how she could remain hopeful, I would respond with the question "What does hope look like for you?" This would begin my spiritual assessment. Is all her hope based on *Hope-that* a treatment would conquer this relentless disease? Does she describe any concepts of *Hope-in*? What gives her a sense of meaning in her life? Did she grow up in a faith tradition? What role does her faith tradition have for her now? Is it comforting or unsettling? What about *Hope-with*? How is her support system? And finally, is she able to experience *Hope-in-the-present-moment*? Is she able to find peace despite her suffering? Is she able to find peace in the stillness of being in the moment she is in without thinking about her past or her future?

As our conversation would unfold, I would be better able to guide Abby on ways to seek other dimensions of hope. I recall from our discussions that she had been raised Catholic. We could have explored how she saw her faith now and what elements of her faith tradition gave her comfort (*Hope-in*). I would also suggest ways of being in the present moment through meditation, centering prayer, the visual arts, music, poetry, journaling, and storytelling (*Hope-in-the-present-moment*). Additionally, I would include her husband, family members, and friends in these activities or in a ritual, if appropriate (*Hope-with*). Finally, since finding a successful treatment was most important to her, I would continue to support her *Hope-that* a treatment could be found.

Hope is a foundation that feeds the human spirit. It is my hope that this book will inspire those who work with the dying to discover new ways to feed the human spirit when a cure is no longer an option. When Abby was in the hospital we briefly discussed the possibility of working together again in the future—and so we did. Abby has been my constant inspiration and guide throughout this exploration of hope. Thank you, my dear friend—*Godspeed.*

References

Alcoholics Anonymous (1935) *The Big Book*. New York, NY: Alcoholic Anonymous Word Services, Inc.

Ali, M.M. (2002) *The Holy Quran: Arabic Text, English Translation and Commentary*. Ahmadlyya Anjuman Isha'at Islam Lahore.

Anandarajah, G. and Height, E. (2002) "Spirituality and medical practice: Using the HOPE questions as a practical tool for spiritual assessment." *American Family Physician 63*, 1, 81–88.

Anderson, M. (2003) *Sacred Dying: Creating Rituals for Embracing the End of Life*. New York, NY: Marlowe & Co.

Austin, C.L., Saylor, R. and Finley, P.J. (2017) "Moral distress in physicians and nurses: Impact on professional quality of life and turnover." *Psychological Trauma: Theory, Research, Practice, and Policy 9*, 4: 399–406.

Black, K. (2004) "Musical Gifts for the Worshipping Body." In C. Gilbertson and G. Muilenburg (eds) *Translucence: Religion, the Arts, and Imagination*. Minneapolis, MN: Augsburg Fortress.

Borg, M.J. (1997) *The God We Never Knew: Beyond Dogmatic Religion to a More Authentic Contemporary Faith*. New York, NY: HarperSanFrancisco.

Borg, M.J. (2011) *Speaking Christian: Why Christian Words Have Lost Their Meaning and Power—And How They Can Be Restored.* New York, NY: Harper One.

Borowitz, E.B. (1983) *Choices in Modern Jewish Thought: A Partisan Guide.* New York, NY: Berman House Inc.

Borowitz, E.B. (1984) *Liberal Judaism.* New York, NY: Union of American Hebrew Congregations.

Burket, S. (2018) *Leaving a Personal Legacy.* Available at Available at www.montgomeryhospice.org/education-resources/leaving-personal-legacy, accessed July 5, 2018.

Burrows, M. (2016) "Seeing through words: Poetry as visual art." *Arts: The Arts in Religious and Theological Studies 28,* 1, 39–48.

Capps, D. (1995) *Agents of Hope: A Pastoral Psychology.* Eugene, OR: Wipf and Stock Publishers.

Chittick, W.C. (1992) "Your Sight Today Is Piercing: The Muslim Understanding of Death and Afterlife." In H. Obayashi (ed.) *Death and Afterlife.* New York, NY: Praeger.

Cooper, R.S., Ferguson, A., Bodurtha, J.N. and Smith, T.J. (2014) "AMEN in challenging conversations: Bridging the gaps between faith, hope, and medicine." *Journal of Oncology Practice 10,* 4, e191–195.

De Sola, C. (2001) "And the Word Became Dance: A Theory and Practice of Liturgical Dance." In D. Adams and D. Apostololos-Cappadona (eds) *Dance as Religious Studies.* Eugene, OR: Wipf and Stock.

Doehring, C. (2006) *The Practice of Pastoral Care: A Postmodern Approach.* Louisville, KY: Westminster John Knox Press.

Driver, T.F. (2006) *Liberating Rites, Understanding the Transformative Power of Ritual.* BookSurge LLC.

Eliott, J. (2005) "What Have We Done with Hope? A Brief History." In J. Eliott (ed.) *Interdisciplinary Perspectives on Hope.* New York, NY: Nova Science Publishers, Inc.

Finger Lakes Donor Recovery Network (2016) "Religion and Organ Donation." Available at www.donorrecovery.org/learn/religion-and-organ-donation, accessed June 14, 2018.

Frank, F. (1973) *The Zen of Seeing: Seeing/Drawing as Meditation.* New York, NY: Vintage Books.

Goldenberg, R. (1992) "Bound up in the Bond of Life: Death and Afterlife in the Jewish Tradition." In Hiroshi Obayashi (ed.) *Death and Afterlife.* New York, NY: Praeger.

Grewe, F. (2017) "The soul's legacy: A program designed to help prepare senior adults cope with end-of-life existential distress." *Journal of Health Care Chaplaincy 23*, 1–14.

Groopman, J. (2004) *The Anatomy of Hope: How People Prevail in The Face of Illness.* New York, NY: Random House.

Guroian, V. (2012) "Learning How to Die Well: Lessons from the Ancient Church." in M.T. Lysaught and J.J. Kolva Jr. (eds) *On Moral Medicine: Theological Perspectives in Medical Ethics* (3rd edn). Grand Rapids, MI: William B. Eerdmans Publishing Co.

Hanh, T.N. (2007) *Living Buddha, Living Christ.* New York, NY: Riverhead Books.

Hick, J. (1994) *Death and Eternal Life.* Louisville, KY: Westminster/John Knox Press.

Hick, J. (2010) *Evil and the God of Love.* Basingstoke: Palgrave Macmillan.

Isay, D. (2007) *Listening Is an Act of Love: A Celebration of American Life from the StoryCorps Project.* New York, NY: The Penguin Press.

Jacobson, L. (2007) *Journey into Now.* La Selva Beach, CA: Conscious Living Publications.

Jacobson, L. (2015) *Words from Silence.* La Selva Beach,, CA: Conscious Living Publications.

Kabat-Zinn, J. (1994) *Wherever You Go, There You Are: Mindfulness Meditation in Everyday Life.* New York, NY: Hyperion.

Keating, T. (2002) *Open Mind, Open Heart: The Contemplative Dimension of the Gospel.* New York, NY: Continuum Publishing Co.

Kertzer, M.N. (1993) *What Is a Jew?* New York, NY: Simon & Schuster.

Krause, N., Emmons, R. and Ironson, G. (2015) "Benevolent Images of God, Gratitude and Physical Status." *Journal of Religion and Health 54*, 1503–1519.

Kubler-Ross, E. (1969) *On Death and Dying.* New York, NY: Scribner.

Lamm, M. (1969) *The Jewish Way of Death and Mourning.* New York, NY: Jonathan David Publishers.

Lamm, M. (1995) *The Power of Hope: The One Essential of Life and Love.* New York, NY: Simon and Schuster.

Lester, A.D. (1995) *Hope in Pastoral Care and Counseling.* Louisville, KY: Westminster John Knox Press.

Levine, S. (1982) *Who Dies? An Investigation of Conscious Living and Conscious Dying.* New York, NY: Anchor Books.

Martin, T.C. (2016) "Flesh made word: Writing as an act of incarnation." *Arts: The Arts in Religious and Theological Studies 28,* 1, 61–71.

McColman, C. (2010) *The Big Book of Christian Mysticism: The Essential Guide to Contemplative Spirituality.* Charlottesville, VA: Hampton Roads Publishing Co.

McDowell, R. (2008) *Poetry as Spiritual Practice: Reading, Writing, and Using Poetry in Your Daily Rituals, Aspirations, and Intentions.* New York, NY: Free Press.

McEntyre, M.C. (2012) "The hope in the waiting." *Weavings: A Journal of the Christian Spiritual Life 27,* 2, 10–15.

McSherry, W. and Cash, K. (2004) "The language of spirituality: An emerging taxonomy." *International Journal of Nursing Studies 41,* 151–161.

Merton, T. (1960) *Spiritual Direction and Meditation.* Collegeville, MN: The Liturgical Press.

Merton, T. (1990) *Contemplative Prayer.* New York, NY: Image Books Doubleday.

Moltmann, J. (1967) *Theology of Hope.* New York, NY: Harper & Row.

Moltmann, J. (1975) *The Experiment Hope.* Philadelphia, NY: Fortress Press.

Moltmann, J. (1977) *The Church in the Power of the Spirit.* New York, NY: Harper & Row Publishers.

Moltmann-Wendel, E. (1995) *I Am My Body: A Theology of Embodiment.* New York, NY: The Continuum Publishing Co.

Mohrmann, M.E. (2012) "Stories and Suffering." In M.T. Lysaught and J.J. Kolva Jr. (eds) *On Moral Medicine: Theological Perspectives in Medical Ethics* (3rd edn). Grand Rapids, MI: William B. Eerdmans Publishing Co.

Morwood, M. (2007) *From Sand to Solid Ground: Questions of Faith for Modern Catholics.* New York, NY: The Crossroad Publishing Co.

Morwood, M. (2013) *It's Time: Challenges to the Doctrine of the Faith.* Kelmor Publishing (www.kelmorpublishing.com).

Nolan, S. (2012) *Spiritual Care at the End of Life: The Chaplin as a Hopeful Presence.* London: Jessica Kingsley Publishers.

Norris, D. (2017) *In the Flow: Passion, Purpose and the Power of Mindfulness.* North Charleston, SC: CreateSpace.

Prestin, A. (2013) "The pursuit of hopefulness: Operationalizing hope in entertainment media narratives." *Media Psychology 16,* 318–345.

Puchalski, C.M. (2006) *A Time for Listening and Caring: Spirituality and the Care of the Chronically Ill and Dying.* New York, NY: Oxford University Press.

Ritchey, K. (2015) "Religion and Public Life, Religious Landscape Study." Pew Research Center, May 12, 2015. Available at www.pewforum. org/2015/05/12/new-pew-research-center-study-examines-americas-changing-religious-landscape, accessed June 14, 2018.

Rohr, R. (2016) "Daily Meditations: The Second Coming of Christ." Available at https://cac.org/second-coming-christ-2016-10-30, accessed June 14, 2018.

Rohr, R. (n.d.) "Poetry and Religion, Daily Meditations." Available at https:// cac.org/category/daily-meditations, accessed June 14, 2018.

Rumbold, B.D. (1986) *Helplessness and Hope: Pastoral Care in Terminal Illness.* London: SCM Press.

Saguil, A. and Phelps, K. (2012) "The spiritual assessment," *American Family Physician 86,* 6, 546–550.

Segal, A. F. (2004) *Life after Death: A History of the Afterlife in Western Religion.* New York, NY: Doubleday.

Siedell, D.A. (2008) *God in the Gallery: A Christian Embrace of Modern Art.* Grand Rapids, MI: Baker Academic.

Singh, K.D. (1982) *The Grace in Dying: A Message of Hope, Comfort, and Spiritual Transformation.* New York, NY: Harper One.

Smith, S.M. (2012) *Caring Liturgies: The Pastoral Power of Christian Ritual.* Minneapolis: MN: Fortress Press.

Sokolove, D. (2013) *Sanctifying Art.* Eugene, OR: Cascade Books.

Steinhauser, K.E. *et al.* (2017) "State of the science of spirituality and palliative care research part 1: Definitions, measurement, and outcomes." *Journal of Pain and Symptom Management 54*, 3, 428–453.

Stone, H.W. and Duke, J,O. (2013) *How to Think Theologically* (3rd edn). Minneapolis, MN: Augsburg Fortress, 2013.

Sumegi, A. (2014) *Understanding Death: An Introduction to Ideas of Self and the Afterlife in World Religions.* Chichester: Wiley Blackwell.

The Holy Bible (1989) *New Revised Standard Version with the Apocrypha.* New York, NY: Harper Bibles.

Tillich, P. (1956) *The Eternal Now.* New York, NY: Charles Scribner's Sons.

Willis, C.B. (2013) *Lasting Words: A Guide to Finding Meaning toward the Close of Life.* Brattleboro, VT: Green Writers Press.

Yates, W. (2015) "Theology and the arts after seventy years: Toward a dialogical approach." *Arts: The Arts in Religious and Theological Studies 26*, 3, 34–42.

Index